Money Smarts

DEFINITIVE TEXTBOOK

Dan Kost

Copyright 2023, 2025

Money Smarts (Vol. 1)

ISBN eBook 978-0-916539-01-6

ISBN Paperback 978-0-916539-02-3

ISBN Hardcover: 978-0-916539-03-0

Printed in United States of America

Disclaimer

The information contained in *Money Smarts (Vol. 1 & Vol. 2)* is for educational purposes only. The author and publisher do not provide legal, financial, or professional advice and make no representations as to the accuracy, completeness, or suitability of the content. While every effort has been made to provide accurate and up-to-date information, readers should consult with a licensed professional for advice tailored to their individual needs.

The author and publisher shall not be held responsible for any errors or omissions in the content, or for any damages resulting from the use of this book. All information is provided "as is," and any reliance placed on such information is at the reader's own risk.

Table of Contents

Chapter 1: Banking   7
  Part 1: Basics of Banking   7
    Opening a bank account: 9
  Part 2: Aspects of Bank Accounts   13
    Bank Accounts: 13
    How to build up your bank account: 16
    Overdraft Fees: 17
    How inflation affects a bank account: 17
    Alert Services and Finance: 18
  Part 3: Types of Accounts   21
    Money Market Accounts: 21
    Certificates of Deposit: 22
    Savings Accounts: 22
    Checking Accounts: 23
    Difference between a credit union and a bank: 24
  Part 4: Currencies   26
    History of Currency: 26
    So what specifically is the US Dollar?:   27
    Types of currency: 28
    Coinage: 29
    Bullion: 29
    Fiat Currency: 30
    Checks: 31
    Money Orders: 32
    Counterfeit Currency: 33
Chapter 2: Bankruptcy   36
  Part 1: Individual Bankruptcy   40
  Part 2: Business Bankruptcy   45
  Part 3: Defaulting   48
    Comparing bankruptcy to defaulting: 49
  Part 4: Debt Relief   51
Chapter 3: Credit   55

Part 1: Credit Building   56

Part 2: Credit Card   58

Pitfalls of having a credit card: 59

Part 3: Credit Reporting   61

Part 4: Credit Repair   65

Chapter 4: Insurance   69

Part 1: Types of Insurance   74

Health Insurance: 75

Life Insurance: 76

Auto Insurance: 78

Automobile Accidents: 79

Automobile Safety: 82

Homeowner's Insurance: 85

Travel Insurance: 86

Liability Insurance: 87

Part 2: Healthcare   89

Part 3: VA Benefits   96

Chapter 5: Loans   104

Cost of Money: 108

Hidden Fees: 110

Part 1: Types of Loans   112

Secured Loan: 112

Unsecured Loans: 113

Revolving Loans: 113

Installment Loans: 114

Payday Loans: 115

Student Loans: 116

Business Loans: 117

Part 2: Uses of Loans   119

Car Loans: 119

Personal Loans: 122

Student Loans: 124

Mortgages: 128

Part 3: Interest   131

Chapter 6: Investing   137

Part 1: Types of Investment   140

Stocks: 140

Bonds: 141

Mutual Funds: 142

Exchange-Traded Funds: 143

Real Estate Investing: 144

Commodity Investing: 145

Futures: 146

Part 2: Interest in Investing   148

Part 3: Positive Collections   154

Blue Chip Companies: 155

Dividend-Paying Companies: 156

Part 4: Cryptocurrency   158

Part 5: AI   162

Part 6: NFTs   169

Chapter 7: Moving toward the Path to Financial Success   176

About the Author   178

Index: 180

Chapter 1: Banking

Part 1: Basics of Banking

Banking refers to the industry, system, and process of managing money and financial transactions. Some of the key aspects of banking include:

1. Deposits: Banks accept deposits from customers, which can include savings accounts, checking accounts, and certificates of deposit (CDs).

2. Loans: Banks provide loans to customers, including personal loans, mortgages, and business loans.

3. Investments: Banks offer investment services such as buying and selling securities, managing portfolios, and offering financial advice.

4. Transactions: Banks facilitate financial transactions between customers and other institutions or individuals, such as wire transfers and electronic payments.

5. Credit: Banks assess the creditworthiness of customers and provide credit in the form of credit cards and lines of credit.

6. Risk management: Banks manage risks associated with lending, investments, and other financial activities, including credit risk, market risk, and operational risk.

7. Regulation: Banks are subject to regulation by government agencies to ensure safety and soundness and protect consumers.

Overall, banking plays a crucial role in the economy by providing financial services that enable individuals and businesses to save, invest, and access credit.

Banking is a financial system that involves the creation of money through the issuance of loans and the management of financial transactions. Banks serve as intermediaries between customers and financial markets, offering a variety of services such as deposit accounts, loans, payment processing, and investment management.

The primary function of a bank is to accept deposits from customers and use those funds to make loans to other customers. When a customer takes out a loan, they pay interest to the bank, which is how the bank makes a profit. Banks also earn money through fees charged for services such as overdraft protection and account maintenance.

To ensure the stability of the financial system and protect customers' deposits, banks are regulated by government agencies and are required to maintain a certain level of reserves and follow strict lending standards. Additionally, deposit accounts at banks are typically insured by government-backed deposit insurance programs.

In summary, banking is a crucial part of the modern economy, providing essential services and stability to individuals, businesses, and the financial system as a whole.

Individual banking refers to the financial services that banks offer to individuals or households. These services can include:

1. Checking and savings accounts: These accounts allow individuals to deposit and withdraw money, pay bills, and earn interest on savings.

2. Loans: Banks offer various types of loans to individuals, including personal loans, car loans, and mortgages.

3. Credit cards: Credit cards allow individuals to make purchases on credit and pay back the balance with interest.

4. Investment services: Banks provide investment services such as buying and selling securities, managing portfolios, and offering financial advice.

5. Retirement planning: Banks can help individuals plan for retirement by offering retirement accounts such as IRAs and 401(k)s.

6. Insurance: Some banks offer insurance products such as life insurance, health insurance, and auto insurance.

Individual banking services can vary depending on the bank and the specific needs of the individual. It's important for individuals to compare different banking options and choose the services that best meet their financial goals and needs.

Opening a bank account

To open a bank account, you will typically need to provide the following:

1. A government-issued ID, such as a driver's license or passport
2. Proof of address, such as a utility bill or lease agreement
3. Initial deposit, which can vary depending on the bank and type of account
4. Personal information, such as your name, address, and social security number
5. Some banks may also ask for your employer information and occupation.

You may also need to fill out an application and provide additional documentation depending on the bank and type of account you are opening. Some banks may also perform a credit check.

To open a bank account, the following documents are typically required:

1. Identification documents: A government-issued ID card such as a driver's license, passport, or national ID card is usually required to prove your identity.

2. Proof of Address: To verify your address, the bank may ask for a recent utility bill, rent agreement, or bank statement with your name and address on it.

3. Social Security Number (SSN): If you are a citizen or resident of the United States, you will need to provide your SSN to the bank.

4. Tax Identification Number (TIN): If you are a business or self-employed, you may need to provide a TIN or EIN (Employer Identification Number).

5. Business documents: If you are opening an account for your business, you will need to provide legal documents such as a

business license, articles of incorporation, or partnership
agreement.

6. Initial deposit: The bank may require an initial deposit to open the
   account, so you should be prepared to provide funds to do so.

It's important to note that the specific documents required may vary
depending on the bank and the country where you are opening the
account. It's always a good idea to check with the bank in advance to
confirm their requirements.

Opening a bank account is a straightforward process that typically
involves the following steps:

1. Choose a bank: Research different banks and compare the types
   of accounts they offer, interest rates, fees, and other services.
2. Gather required documents: Most banks will require proof of
   identity, such as a government-issued ID, and proof of address,
   such as a utility bill. You may also need to provide your Social
   Security number.
3. Complete an application: Fill out the bank's account application
   either online, over the phone, or in person.
4. Fund the account: To open an account, you will usually need to
   make an initial deposit, which can be done by cash, check, or
   electronic transfer.
5. Wait for account approval: The bank will review your application
   and may run a credit check to verify your identity and assess any
   potential risks. This process may take several days.
6. Sign up for online banking: Once your account is approved, sign
   up for online banking to access your account information, make
   transactions, and manage your finances from anywhere with an
   internet connection.
7. Receive your debit card: Many banks will issue a debit card
   linked to your account, which you can use to withdraw cash,
   make purchases, and pay bills.

In conclusion, opening a bank account is a straightforward process that
requires choosing a bank, gathering required documents, completing an
application, funding the account, and waiting for approval. With a bank

account, you can manage your finances, make transactions, and access your money easily and securely.

There are several reasons why someone may be denied a bank account. Some common reasons include:

1. Insufficient identification: The bank may require additional documentation or may not accept the form of identification provided.
2. Checkered credit history: Banks may run a credit check before opening an account, and if the individual has a poor credit history, they may be denied.
3. Past banking issues: If an individual has a history of unpaid debts, bounced checks, or other banking issues, they may be denied a new account.
4. Illegal activities: Banks are required to comply with laws and regulations, so if an individual is involved in illegal activities such as money laundering, they may be denied an account.
5. OFAC List: If the individual's name is listed on the Office of Foreign Assets Control (OFAC) list of Specially Designated Nationals (SDN) or other restricted lists, they will be denied an account.
6. Non-compliance with AML/KYC: Banks also have to comply with Anti Money Laundering (AML) and Know Your Customer (KYC) regulations, if the individual is not able to provide the required information or if the information provided is suspicious, the bank may deny the account.

Part 2: Aspects of Bank Accounts

Bank Accounts

A bank account is a financial account that is offered by a bank or other financial institution to its customers. It allows the account holder to deposit, withdraw, and manage their money in a safe and secure manner. Bank accounts come in various types, including checking accounts, savings accounts, money market accounts, and certificates of deposit (CDs).

Checking accounts are designed for everyday transactions, such as paying bills, making purchases, and withdrawing cash from ATMs. They often come with a debit card that can be used for purchases and cash withdrawals.

Savings accounts, on the other hand, are designed for long-term saving. They generally offer a higher interest rate than checking accounts, but may have restrictions on how often funds can be withdrawn.

Money market accounts are similar to savings accounts but often offer higher interest rates and more flexibility in terms of withdrawals. They typically require a higher minimum balance than savings accounts.

Certificates of deposit (CDs) are a type of savings account that requires a fixed amount of money to be deposited for a set period of time. CDs typically offer higher interest rates than savings accounts but often have penalties for early withdrawal.

In general, bank accounts provide a safe and convenient way to manage money, earn interest, and access funds when needed. However, it is important to carefully consider the terms and fees associated with different types of accounts to find the one that best suits your financial needs.

Here are the general steps to follow to get a bank account:

1. Determine the type of account you need: Before opening a bank account, it is important to consider your financial needs and

choose the type of account that best suits them. As mentioned earlier, there are various types of bank accounts available, including checking accounts, savings accounts, money market accounts, and certificates of deposit. Each type of account has different features, fees, and minimum balance requirements.

2. Choose a bank or financial institution: Once you have determined the type of account you need, you will need to choose a bank or financial institution that offers that type of account. You can do research online, ask friends and family for recommendations, or visit different banks in person to learn about their offerings.

3. Gather the required documents: To open a bank account, you will typically need to provide personal identification and other documentation. This may include your Social Security number, driver's license or passport, proof of address (such as a utility bill or lease agreement), and proof of income (such as pay stubs or tax returns).

4. Fill out the application: Once you have chosen a bank and gathered the required documents, you will need to fill out an application to open an account. This application will typically ask for personal information such as your name, address, date of birth, and employment status.

5. Make an initial deposit: Many banks require an initial deposit to open a new account. The amount of the deposit varies depending on the type of account and the bank's policies. Some banks may allow you to fund the account with a personal check or transfer from another account, while others may require cash or a certified check.

6. Review and sign the account agreement: Before the account is opened, you will be provided with an account agreement that outlines the terms and conditions of the account, including any fees or charges. Review the agreement carefully and ask questions if you have any concerns. Once you are satisfied, sign the agreement to open the account.

7. Activate your account: Once the account is opened, you will typically receive a debit card and/or checks in the mail within a few business days. Follow the instructions provided to activate your account and start using it for your financial needs.

It is important to note that the specific steps and requirements for opening a bank account may vary depending on the bank or financial institution, as well as your personal circumstances. It is always a good idea to do your research and ask questions before opening a new account.

While bank accounts offer many benefits, there are also some potential pitfalls that consumers should be aware of:

1. Fees: Many banks charge fees for various account services, such as ATM use, overdrafts, and monthly maintenance. These fees can add up and eat into your account balance if you are not careful. It is important to read the terms and conditions of your account carefully to understand the fees that may apply and how to avoid them.
2. Fraud: Bank accounts can be vulnerable to fraud, such as identity theft, phishing scams, and other types of cybercrime. It is important to monitor your account regularly for unauthorized transactions and take steps to protect your personal information and account access.
3. Limited access to funds: Some types of bank accounts, such as certificates of deposit and money market accounts, may have restrictions on when and how you can access your funds. It is important to understand the terms of your account and plan accordingly to avoid being caught without access to your money when you need it.
4. Inflation: While bank accounts offer a low-risk way to save money, they may not offer the same level of return as other types of investments. Over time, inflation can erode the value of your savings and make it harder to achieve your financial goals.
5. Account closures: Banks may close your account for various reasons, such as inactivity, overdrafts, or suspicious activity. If your account is closed, you may be unable to access your funds or may face additional fees and charges.

To avoid these pitfalls, it is important to choose a reputable bank or financial institution, read the terms and conditions of your account carefully, monitor your account regularly, and take steps to protect your personal information and account access. Additionally, it can be helpful to regularly review your financial goals and needs to ensure that your account choices are aligned with your overall financial plan.

How to build up your bank account

Building up currency typically involves saving money over time and making smart financial decisions to increase your wealth. Here are some strategies that can help you build up your currency:

1. Budgeting: Creating a budget can help you track your expenses and identify areas where you can cut back on spending. By reducing unnecessary expenses, you can free up more money to save or invest.

2. Saving: Setting aside a portion of your income each month can help you build up your savings over time. You can automate your savings by setting up automatic transfers from your checking account to a savings account.

3. Investing: Investing your money in stocks, bonds, real estate, or other assets can help you grow your wealth over time. However, it's important to understand the risks and do your research before investing your money.

4. Earning more: Increasing your income by taking on a side job or starting a business can help you build up your currency faster. You can also negotiate for a higher salary or look for job opportunities that offer better pay and benefits.

5. Paying off debt: Paying off high-interest debt, such as credit card balances, can help you save money on interest and free up more money for saving and investing.

6. Being disciplined: Building up currency takes time and discipline. It's important to stick to your budget, avoid unnecessary expenses, and stay focused on your long-term financial goals.

Overall, building up currency requires a combination of smart financial decisions, discipline, and patience. By following these strategies, you can increase your wealth and achieve your financial goals over time.

Overdraft Fees

Overdraft fees are fees charged by banks and financial institutions when you make a transaction that exceeds the available balance in your account. For example, if you have $100 in your checking account and make a purchase for $150, you may be charged an overdraft fee.

Overdraft fees can vary depending on the bank and the type of account you have. Some banks may charge a flat fee for each overdraft transaction, while others may charge a percentage of the overdrawn amount. Additionally, some banks may have daily limits on the number of overdraft fees they will charge.

Overdraft fees can be costly and can quickly add up if you frequently overdraw your account. In addition to the overdraft fee, you may also be charged additional fees or interest if you do not bring your account back into a positive balance within a certain timeframe.

To avoid overdraft fees, it is important to monitor your account balance regularly and keep track of your transactions. You may also be able to sign up for overdraft protection, which can help prevent overdrafts by linking your checking account to another account, such as a savings account or line of credit.

If you do incur overdraft fees, it is important to take action to avoid future fees. This may include setting up account alerts, setting up a budget, or speaking with your bank to explore other options for managing your finances.

How inflation affects a bank account

Inflation is the rate at which the general level of prices for goods and services in an economy is increasing. When inflation occurs, the purchasing power of money decreases over time, meaning that the same amount of money can buy fewer goods and services than it could previously. This can have several effects on a bank account:

1. Interest rates: Inflation can lead to higher interest rates, which can be beneficial for savings accounts and other interest-bearing accounts. When inflation is high, banks may raise their interest rates to encourage people to save their money and reduce spending. This can help account holders earn more interest on their savings and potentially keep up with the rate of inflation.
2. Purchasing power: Inflation can reduce the purchasing power of money held in a bank account. If the rate of inflation is higher than the interest rate earned on the account, the account holder's money may lose value over time. For example, if inflation is 2% and the interest rate on a savings account is 1%, the account holder's money is effectively losing value at a rate of 1% per year.
3. Loan repayments: Inflation can also affect loan repayments. If inflation is high, the value of the money used to repay a loan may be less than the value of the money borrowed. This can be beneficial for borrowers, as they may be able to pay back their loans with less valuable money. However, it can be harmful for lenders, as they may not be able to keep up with the rate of inflation and may lose money on the loan.

Overall, inflation can have both positive and negative effects on a bank account. While higher interest rates can be beneficial for savings accounts, inflation can also reduce the purchasing power of money held in the account. Additionally, inflation can affect loan repayments and potentially harm lenders.

Alert Services and Finance

Alert services are a type of notification system that provides users with updates or alerts about specific events, conditions, or information. These services are designed to keep users informed in real-time, often through a variety of channels such as email, SMS, push notifications, or social media.

Alert services can be used for a wide range of purposes, including:

1. Security alerts: These alerts inform users about potential security threats such as unauthorized access to their accounts, or suspicious activity on their devices or networks.

2. Weather alerts: These alerts inform users about severe weather conditions, such as hurricanes, tornadoes, or other natural disasters.

3. Financial alerts: These alerts inform users about changes in the financial markets, fluctuations in stock prices, or changes in their account balances.

4. Health alerts: These alerts inform users about changes in their health status, reminders for medication, or upcoming appointments.

5. News alerts: These alerts inform users about breaking news stories or updates on specific topics of interest.

6. Social media alerts: These alerts inform users about activity on their social media accounts, such as new followers, likes, or comments.

Alert services can be customized to fit the specific needs of the user, allowing them to choose the type of alerts they receive, the frequency of the alerts, and the channels through which they are delivered. This level of customization helps to ensure that users are only receiving relevant information, and not inundated with irrelevant alerts that can be a distraction.

Yes, alert services can be particularly useful for monitoring and managing finances. There are several types of financial alerts that can be set up to keep users informed about their financial status and transactions.

1. Account balance alerts: These alerts can be set up to notify users when their account balance drops below a certain threshold or reaches a specific level. This can help users avoid overdraft fees or prevent fraudulent transactions.

2. Transaction alerts: These alerts can be set up to notify users when transactions are made on their account, such as purchases, withdrawals, or deposits. This can help users monitor their spending and quickly detect any unauthorized transactions.

3. Bill payment alerts: These alerts can be set up to notify users when bills are due or when payments have been made. This can help users avoid late fees and ensure that bills are paid on time.

4. Credit score alerts: These alerts can be set up to notify users when there are changes to their credit score or credit report. This can help users monitor their creditworthiness and detect any errors or fraudulent activity.

By using financial alert services, users can stay on top of their finances and make informed decisions about their money. These services can provide peace of mind, help users avoid unnecessary fees, and prevent fraudulent activity.

Part 3: Types of Accounts

Money Market Accounts

A money market account is a type of deposit account offered by banks and other financial institutions that typically pays a higher interest rate than a traditional savings account. It is similar to a savings account, but with a few key differences.

First, money market accounts often require a higher minimum balance than savings accounts. This minimum balance requirement can range from a few hundred to several thousand dollars. In exchange for maintaining a higher balance, account holders are typically rewarded with a higher interest rate.

Second, money market accounts typically limit the number of transactions that can be made each month. This is to encourage account holders to use the account for saving rather than for everyday spending. Transactions may include checks, debit card purchases, and electronic transfers.

Money market accounts are a good option for those who want to earn a higher interest rate on their savings while still having relatively easy access to their funds. They are generally considered to be a low-risk investment, as they are FDIC insured up to the maximum allowed by law.

However, it is important to note that money market accounts may have higher fees or require a higher minimum balance than other types of deposit accounts. Additionally, the interest rate on a money market account can fluctuate depending on market conditions, so it is important to carefully consider the account terms and do research before opening an account.

Overall, money market accounts can be a good option for those who want to earn a higher interest rate on their savings while still having relatively easy access to their funds.

Certificates of Deposit

Certificates of deposit (CDs) are a type of deposit account offered by banks and other financial institutions that offer a fixed rate of interest for a set period of time. They are often used as a low-risk investment vehicle for people who want to save money for a specific purpose, such as a down payment on a house or a child's college tuition.

When you open a CD, you agree to deposit a fixed amount of money for a specified term, which can range from a few months to several years. The interest rate on the CD is generally higher than the interest rate on a savings account, but it is fixed for the entire term of the CD.

One advantage of CDs is that they are FDIC insured up to the maximum allowed by law, which means that the money you deposit in a CD is protected against bank failure. Another advantage is that CDs offer a predictable return on investment, which can be helpful for people who want to budget their finances.

However, there are also some disadvantages to consider. For example, if you need to withdraw your money before the end of the CD term, you may be subject to penalties or forfeit some of the interest earned. Additionally, if interest rates rise during the term of the CD, you will not be able to take advantage of the higher rates until the CD matures.

When considering a CD, it is important to shop around for the best interest rates and terms. Some banks and credit unions offer higher rates for longer terms, while others may offer promotions or special rates for new customers. It is also important to consider your financial goals and needs to determine if a CD is the right investment choice for you.

Savings Accounts

A savings account is a type of deposit account offered by banks and other financial institutions that allows individuals to save money and earn interest on their deposits. Savings accounts are often used as a tool for individuals to set aside funds for emergencies, future expenses, or long-term goals.

One of the primary advantages of a savings account is that it is a low-risk investment. Savings accounts are FDIC insured up to the maximum allowed by law, which means that the money you deposit in a savings account is protected against bank failure. Additionally, savings accounts typically offer a modest interest rate, which can help your savings grow over time.

Another advantage of a savings account is that it offers relatively easy access to your money. While savings accounts may have some limitations on the number of transactions you can make each month, you can generally withdraw your money without penalty or restriction.

However, there are also some disadvantages to consider. For example, savings accounts typically have lower interest rates than other types of investment vehicles, such as stocks or bonds. Additionally, inflation can erode the purchasing power of your savings over time, so it is important to consider the impact of inflation when setting savings goals.

When choosing a savings account, it is important to shop around for the best interest rates and terms. Some banks and credit unions offer higher rates or special promotions for new customers. Additionally, it is important to consider your financial goals and needs to determine if a savings account is the right choice for you.

Checking Accounts

A checking account is a type of deposit account offered by banks and other financial institutions that allows individuals to deposit and withdraw money as needed to pay bills, make purchases, and manage day-to-day finances. Checking accounts typically come with a variety of features and benefits, including a debit card, check-writing privileges, and online banking.

One of the primary advantages of a checking account is that it offers easy access to your money. With a checking account, you can make transactions and access your funds quickly and easily using a debit card, online banking, or mobile banking. Additionally, many checking accounts offer features such as overdraft protection, which can help you avoid costly fees and charges if you accidentally overdraw your account.

Another advantage of a checking account is that it allows you to keep your money safe and secure. Checking accounts are FDIC insured up to the maximum allowed by law, which means that the money you deposit in a checking account is protected against bank failure. Additionally, many banks and financial institutions offer fraud protection and other security features to help keep your account safe from unauthorized access or transactions.

However, there are also some potential drawbacks to consider. For example, some checking accounts may have fees or charges associated with certain transactions or account features. Additionally, some banks and financial institutions may require a minimum balance or impose other restrictions on your account.

When choosing a checking account, it is important to consider your financial goals and needs, as well as the fees, charges, and other features of the account. Shopping around for the best account can help you find the account that best meets your needs and helps you achieve your financial goals.

Difference between a credit union and a bank

Credit unions and banks are both financial institutions that offer a variety of financial services, such as checking and savings accounts, loans, and credit cards. However, there are several key differences between the two:

1. Ownership: Banks are for-profit institutions, owned by shareholders who expect to earn a return on their investment. Credit unions, on the other hand, are non-profit institutions owned by their members, who are also their customers. This means that credit unions are often able to offer lower fees and better interest rates than banks, since they do not have to generate profits for shareholders.
2. Membership: Banks are open to anyone who meets their eligibility requirements and can meet the minimum account balance requirements. Credit unions, however, have membership criteria that must be met, such as working for a particular employer or belonging to a specific community or organization.
3. Products and services: Banks generally offer a wide range of financial products and services, including mortgages, credit cards, and business loans. Credit unions typically have a smaller range of products and services, but may offer more personalized service and better rates on certain products, such as auto loans and mortgages.

4. Fees and charges: Banks may charge higher fees and interest rates on loans and credit cards than credit unions, as they are focused on generating profits for shareholders. Credit unions may also offer fee waivers and other incentives to members to encourage loyalty and reduce costs.
5. Regulation: Banks are regulated by federal and state agencies, such as the Federal Reserve and the FDIC, while credit unions are regulated by the National Credit Union Administration (NCUA). The NCUA is an independent federal agency that oversees and insures credit unions, similar to the FDIC for banks.

Overall, the main difference between a credit union and a bank is their ownership structure and focus on profits. While both types of institutions offer similar services, credit unions may offer more personalized service, lower fees, and better interest rates for their members.

Part 4: Currencies

Currency refers to a system of money in use in a particular country or region. It is a medium of exchange that is used to facilitate transactions for goods and services, as well as for payment of debts and taxes.

The most common types of currency include banknotes and coins, which are issued by the government or central bank of a country. These physical forms of currency represent a certain value and can be exchanged for goods and services.

In addition to physical currency, there is also digital currency, which is a form of currency that is stored electronically and used for transactions online. Examples of digital currency include cryptocurrencies like Bitcoin and Ethereum, which are decentralized and operate independently of traditional banking systems.

The value of currency is determined by a variety of factors, including supply and demand, economic policies, inflation, and international trade. Currency exchange rates also play a crucial role in determining the value of a currency in relation to other currencies, and these rates can fluctuate based on market conditions and economic indicators.

Overall, currency is a vital component of modern economies and plays a significant role in facilitating trade and commerce both domestically and internationally.

History of Currency

The use of currency can be traced back to ancient civilizations, with evidence of coins and other forms of currency dating as far back as 600 BC. The earliest forms of currency were often made from precious metals such as gold, silver, and bronze and were used to facilitate trade and commerce.

In ancient times, the value of currency was often determined by the weight and purity of the metal used, with coins and bars being stamped with images and inscriptions to indicate their origin and value. Over time, different regions developed their own unique currencies, and trade between these regions became more complex, leading to the development of international currency exchange.

During the Middle Ages, paper money began to emerge as a form of currency in China and other parts of Asia. This early paper money was backed by precious metals and was used to facilitate long-distance trade and commerce.

In the 17th and 18th centuries, European colonial powers began to establish global trading networks, and currencies like the Spanish dollar became widely used in international trade. The first modern central banks were also established during this time, as governments sought to regulate and control the supply of currency in their respective economies.

In the 20th century, the use of paper money became more widespread, and new technologies such as electronic banking and digital currencies began to emerge. Today, the world's major currencies include the US dollar, the Euro, the Japanese yen, and the British pound, and currency exchange markets play a crucial role in facilitating global trade and commerce.

Throughout history, the use of currency has evolved to meet the changing needs of society, and it will continue to do so as new technologies and economic systems emerge.

So what specifically is the US Dollar?

The United States dollar (USD) is the official currency of the United States and its territories. It is also widely used as a reserve currency and as a medium of international exchange by many countries around the world. The dollar is divided into 100 smaller units called cents.

The value of the dollar is determined by supply and demand in the foreign exchange market. The US dollar is considered a safe-haven currency, meaning that it is in high demand during times of economic uncertainty, and its value tends to increase as a result.

The US dollar is issued and controlled by the Federal Reserve System, also known as the "Fed." The Fed is the central bank of the United States and is responsible for conducting monetary policy, regulating the supply of money, and supervising banks.

Since the end of the gold standard in 1971, the US dollar has been a purely fiat currency, meaning that it is not convertible into gold or any other physical asset. Instead, the value of the US dollar is determined by supply and demand in the foreign exchange markets, as well as by the policies of the US government and the Federal Reserve.

In summary, the United States dollar is a crucial currency both domestically and globally, serving as a medium of exchange and a store of value for individuals, businesses, and governments.

Types of currency

Currency refers to physical money, such as coins and paper bills, that is issued by a government and used as a medium of exchange for goods and services.

A check is a written order to a financial institution, usually a bank, to pay a specified amount of money to a specified person or entity. The check is drawn on the writer's account and serves as a form of payment.

A money order is a prepaid certificate or receipt that acts as a substitute for cash. It is often used for transactions when cash or a personal check is not accepted. Money orders are typically sold by financial institutions, post offices, and other businesses, and they are often used for rent payments, bill payments, and other types of payments that require a secure and trusted form of payment.

Both checks and money orders serve as a form of payment, but money orders are considered more secure as they are prepaid and less susceptible to fraudulent use. In contrast, checks can be forged or altered, which makes them a less secure form of payment.

Coinage

Coins are small, flat, and usually round pieces of metal that are used as a form of currency. Coins have been used for thousands of years as a means of exchange, and they continue to be used in many countries around the world today.

Coins are typically issued by governments and have a specific face value that is printed or stamped on them. The value of a coin is determined by the government that issues it and is usually based on the weight and composition of the metal used to make the coin.

Coins are typically used for small transactions, such as purchasing food or beverages from a vending machine, paying for public transportation, or making small purchases at a store. In some countries, coins are also used as a form of collectible currency, with rare or unique coins being highly sought after by collectors.

Coins come in various denominations, depending on the country and the currency system in use. For example, in the United States, coins are issued in denominations of 1 cent, 5 cents, 10 cents, 25 cents, 50 cents, and 1 dollar. In other countries, such as the United Kingdom, coins are issued in denominations of 1 penny, 2 pence, 5 pence, 10 pence, 20 pence, 50 pence, and 1 pound.

Overall, coins continue to be an important form of currency around the world, providing a convenient and durable means of exchange for small transactions.

Bullion

Bullion refers to a form of precious metal, such as gold, silver, platinum, or palladium, that is cast in bars or coins of a standardized weight and purity. These metals are typically considered to be valuable and are often used as a store of wealth or as an investment.

Bullion can be purchased in a variety of forms, including bars, coins, and rounds. The weight and purity of bullion are typically expressed in troy ounces or grams, with the weight often ranging from 1 gram to several hundred ounces.

One of the primary uses of bullion is as a hedge against inflation and economic uncertainty. Because the value of precious metals is generally seen as stable or even increasing over time, investors often turn to bullion as a way to protect their wealth during times of economic volatility or inflation.

In addition to its use as an investment, bullion also has industrial applications, particularly in the electronics, medical, and automotive industries. For example, gold is used in the production of computer chips and other electronic components, while platinum is used in catalytic converters in automobiles.

Bullion is often bought and sold through dealers or brokers, who specialize in the trade of precious metals. The price of bullion can fluctuate based on a variety of factors, including supply and demand, economic conditions, and geopolitical events.

Overall, bullion serves as a tangible asset that can be bought and sold for its intrinsic value, making it a popular choice for investors and collectors alike.

Fiat Currency

A fiat currency is a type of currency that is issued by a government and is not backed by a physical commodity such as gold or silver. Instead, the value of a fiat currency is based on the trust and confidence that people have in the issuing government and the currency itself.

Fiat currencies are typically issued in paper or digital form and are accepted as a medium of exchange for goods and services. The value of a fiat currency is determined by supply and demand, and can be influenced by a number of factors such as interest rates, economic conditions, and government policies.

One of the key features of fiat currencies is that they are not redeemable for a fixed amount of a physical commodity. This allows governments to issue more currency as needed, which can help to stimulate economic activity, but can also lead to inflation if too much currency is introduced into circulation.

In summary, fiat currencies are a type of currency that is not backed by a physical commodity and is based on the trust and confidence in the issuing government and the currency itself.

Checks

A check is a written document that instructs a bank or financial institution to pay a specified amount of money to the person or organization named on the check. Checks are a commonly used form of payment for a variety of transactions, including payment of bills, purchasing goods and services, and transferring money between accounts.

To write a check, the person or organization making the payment fills out the necessary information on the check, including the date, the name of the person or organization receiving the payment (the payee), the amount of money to be paid in both words and numbers, and the signature of the account holder. The check also includes the bank account number and routing number associated with the account from which the payment is being made.

When the payee receives the check, they can deposit it into their own bank account, and the money will be transferred from the account of the person or organization making the payment. Checks can take several days to clear, during which time the bank will verify that the account has sufficient funds to cover the payment.

Checks have been used as a form of payment for centuries and remain a popular method of payment despite the rise of electronic payment methods such as credit cards and online payments. However, checks can be vulnerable to fraud, and it is important to take measures to protect against check fraud, such as using secure check stock, reviewing bank statements regularly, and keeping checks and other financial documents in a secure location.

A check is a written order to a financial institution, usually a bank, to pay a specified amount of money to a specified person or entity. Here are the steps to write a check:

1. Date: Write the current date on the top right line.
2. Payee: Write the name of the person or entity you are paying on the "Pay to the Order Of" line.
3. Amount in Numbers: Write the amount you are paying in numbers on the dollar line.
4. Amount in Words: Write the amount you are paying in words on the line below "Pay to the Order Of."
5. Memo: You can use the memo line for a brief description of the purpose of the check, such as "Rent" or "Utilities."
6. Signature: Sign the check on the line at the bottom right

Money Orders

A money order is a type of financial instrument that functions like a check, but it is prepaid with a specific amount of money. Money orders are often used as a safe and convenient way to send and receive payments, particularly for transactions that require more security or that involve sending money through the mail.

To purchase a money order, an individual pays the face value of the money order plus a small fee to the issuer, typically a bank, post office, or other financial institution. The individual then provides the name of the recipient, who can then cash the money order or deposit it into their bank account.

Unlike checks, money orders are prepaid and do not allow for overdrafts or bouncing. Additionally, they are less susceptible to fraud than checks, as they require the purchaser to provide cash up front, rather than relying on a bank account that may not have sufficient funds.

Money orders are also useful for people who do not have a bank account, as they provide a secure and reliable way to send and receive money without the need for a checking account or other financial account. They are also commonly used for transactions that require proof of payment, such as rental deposits or payments for goods and services purchased online.

Overall, money orders provide a convenient and secure way to send and receive money for individuals who may not have access to traditional banking services, or for transactions that require more security than a personal check can provide.

Counterfeit Currency

Counterfeit currency refers to fake or imitation money that is produced with the intention of deceiving others and passing it off as genuine currency. Counterfeit currency can be in the form of banknotes, coins, or digital currency, and it is typically created using materials and equipment that are similar to those used to produce genuine currency.

The production and distribution of counterfeit currency is illegal in most countries, and those caught counterfeiting currency can face severe legal penalties. Counterfeit currency can be used to purchase goods and services, pay debts, and even fund illegal activities such as money laundering and terrorism.

To prevent the circulation of counterfeit currency, governments and central banks take several measures, such as incorporating security features into banknotes and coins that are difficult to reproduce, using specialized printing techniques, and implementing anti-counterfeiting laws and regulations. Additionally, businesses and individuals can take steps to protect themselves from counterfeit currency by familiarizing themselves with the security features of genuine currency and using counterfeit detection devices when handling large amounts of cash.

Counterfeit currency can be a significant threat to the stability of the economy, as it can erode confidence in the value of currency and undermine trust in financial institutions. Therefore, it is crucial for individuals, businesses, and governments to remain vigilant against the production and distribution of counterfeit currency.

Counterfeit currency can have a number of negative effects on individuals, businesses, and the economy as a whole. Here are some of the pitfalls of counterfeit currency:

1. Loss of value: Counterfeit currency can decrease the value of

    legitimate currency by flooding the market with fake bills. When there is more counterfeit currency in circulation, it can lead to inflation, which reduces the purchasing power of consumers and businesses.

2. Financial losses: Individuals and businesses that unknowingly accept counterfeit currency can suffer financial losses when the bills are discovered to be fake. In some cases, businesses may not be reimbursed for their losses if they accepted the counterfeit currency without taking proper precautions.

3. Legal consequences: Using or distributing counterfeit currency is illegal and can result in serious legal consequences, including fines and imprisonment. Individuals or businesses found to be using counterfeit currency may also face damage to their reputation and loss of business.

4. Damage to the economy: Counterfeit currency can damage the economy by reducing consumer and investor confidence in the financial system. This can lead to a decrease in spending and investment, which can have a negative impact on economic growth.

5. Increased security costs: To combat the problem of counterfeit currency, businesses and governments must spend more money on security measures, such as counterfeit detection technology and training for employees. This can be a significant expense for businesses, particularly small businesses.

Overall, counterfeit currency can have a number of negative effects on individuals, businesses, and the economy. It's important for individuals and businesses to be vigilant and take steps to protect themselves against counterfeit currency, such as using counterfeit detection technology and educating themselves on how to spot fake bills.

Chapter 2: Bankruptcy

Bankruptcy is a legal process in which an individual or business is unable to repay their debts as they become due. The purpose of bankruptcy is to provide a fair and orderly process for the resolution of the debtor's outstanding debts. The most common types of bankruptcy for individuals are Chapter 7 and Chapter 13. In Chapter 7, also known as a "liquidation" bankruptcy, the debtor's assets are sold and the proceeds are used to pay off the debtor's creditors. In Chapter 13, also known as a "reorganization" bankruptcy, the debtor's assets are not sold, but the debtor must propose a plan to repay a portion of their debts over a period of 3 to 5 years.

Businesses can file for bankruptcy under Chapter 7 or Chapter 11. Chapter 7 is similar to the process for individuals, in that the business's assets are sold and the proceeds are used to pay off the business's creditors. Chapter 11 is more complex, and is intended for businesses that wish to continue operating while they reorganize their debts. The business will file a plan of reorganization with the court, which must be approved by the court and the business's creditors. The business will then operate under the supervision of the court while it repays its debts.

Filing for bankruptcy can have a significant impact on an individual or business's credit rating and financial future. It is a serious decision and should not be taken lightly. It is recommended that individuals or businesses seeking to file for bankruptcy consult with an attorney who specializes in bankruptcy law.

There are several types of bankruptcy available to individuals and businesses, each with their own specific purpose and eligibility requirements. The most common types of bankruptcy are:

- Chapter 7 bankruptcy: Also known as "liquidation" bankruptcy, this type of bankruptcy is available to individuals, married couples, and some businesses. The purpose of Chapter 7 bankruptcy is to discharge, or eliminate, certain types of unsecured debt, such as credit card debt, medical bills, and personal loans. In Chapter 7, the debtor's assets are sold and the proceeds are used to pay off the debtor's creditors. It's important to note that certain types of debt, such as most taxes, student loans, and fines, are not dischargeable in a Chapter 7 bankruptcy.

- Chapter 13 bankruptcy: Also known as "reorganization" bankruptcy, this type of bankruptcy is available to individuals and married couples who have regular income and a significant amount of debt. Unlike Chapter 7 bankruptcy, which liquidates assets to pay off creditors, Chapter 13 bankruptcy allows the debtor to keep their assets and repay their debts over a period of 3 to 5 years through a repayment plan.

- Chapter 11 bankruptcy: This type of bankruptcy is available to businesses that wish to continue operating while they reorganize their debts. The purpose of Chapter 11 bankruptcy is to allow the business to restructure its debt and operations in order to become financially viable again. The business must propose a plan of reorganization to the court, which must be approved by the court and the business's creditors.

- Chapter 12 bankruptcy: This type of bankruptcy is similar to Chapter 13, but it's designed specifically for family farmers and fishermen. It allows them to repay their debts over a period of 3 to 5 years through a repayment plan.

- Chapter 9 bankruptcy: This type of bankruptcy is available to municipalities, such as cities, towns, and counties, and it allows them to reorganize their debt.

It's important to note that each type of bankruptcy has its own specific eligibility requirements, and that the laws and regulations regarding bankruptcy can vary from state to state. It's always best to consult with a bankruptcy attorney before filing for bankruptcy to get a clear understanding of which type of bankruptcy is best for you or your business and what the process will entail.

Bankruptcy can be a powerful tool for individuals and businesses that are struggling with debt, but it's important to be aware of the potential pitfalls of bankruptcy as well. Some of the most common pitfalls of bankruptcy include:

1. Damage to credit score: Filing for bankruptcy can have a significant impact on your credit score, and it may remain on your credit report for up to 10 years. This can make it difficult to obtain credit, a loan, or a mortgage in the future.

2. Cost: Filing for bankruptcy can be expensive, as you'll need to pay for court fees, lawyer's fees, and other expenses associated with the process.

3. Loss of assets: In a Chapter 7 bankruptcy, you may be required to sell some of your assets in order to pay off your creditors. This can include your home, car, and other valuable possessions.

4. Public record: Bankruptcy is a matter of public record, and the information is available to the public, including future creditors and employers.

5. Lengthy process: The bankruptcy process can be lengthy and complex, and it can take several months to several years to complete, depending on the type of bankruptcy you file and the complexity of your case.

6. Post-bankruptcy debt: While bankruptcy can discharge many types of debt, it's important to be aware that certain types of debt,

such as most taxes, student loans, and fines, cannot be discharged in a bankruptcy.

7. Limited discharge: While bankruptcy can discharge many types of unsecured debt, it's important to be aware that some types of debt, such as alimony, child support, and certain types of judgments, cannot be discharged in a bankruptcy.

It's important to consider these potential pitfalls before filing for bankruptcy and to understand that bankruptcy is not a cure-all solution for financial problems. It's always best to consult with a bankruptcy attorney to understand the benefits and drawbacks of bankruptcy and to determine if it's the right choice for you or your business.

Part 1: Individual Bankruptcy

Chapter 7 bankruptcy, also known as "liquidation" bankruptcy, is a type of bankruptcy available to individuals, married couples, and some businesses. The purpose of Chapter 7 bankruptcy is to discharge, or eliminate, certain types of unsecured debt, such as credit card debt, medical bills, and personal loans.

When an individual files for Chapter 7 bankruptcy, the court will appoint a trustee to oversee the process. The trustee's role is to review the debtor's assets and determine which assets are exempt and which are non-exempt. Exempt assets are typically those that are necessary for the debtor's basic living expenses, such as a primary residence, personal property, and tools of the trade. Non-exempt assets, such as a second home, vacation property, or luxury items, may be sold by the trustee to pay off the debtor's creditors.

The debtor must also submit a list of all their creditors and the amount of money they owe to each one, as well as a schedule of their income and expenses. The debtor must also attend a meeting of creditors, also known as a "341 meeting," where the trustee and creditors can ask the debtor questions about their financial situation.

Once the trustee has reviewed the debtor's assets and determined which assets are non-exempt, the trustee will sell the non-exempt assets and use the proceeds to pay off the debtor's creditors. Any remaining debt that is not dischargeable will have to be paid by the debtor.

It's important to note that certain types of debt, such as most taxes, student loans, and fines, are not dischargeable in a Chapter 7 bankruptcy.

It typically takes around 3-6 months to complete the Chapter 7 process, and once it is completed, the debtor will receive a discharge, which releases them from personal liability for most of their dischargeable debts. However, it's important to note that a bankruptcy filing can have a significant impact on an individual's credit rating, and it will stay in their credit report for up to 10 years.

Under Chapter 7 bankruptcy, certain types of debt can be discharged, which means that the debtor is no longer legally responsible for paying them. These types of debt include:

- Credit card debt
- Medical bills
- Personal loans
- Certain types of judgments
- Some types of business debt

On the other hand, certain types of debt are not dischargeable under Chapter 7 bankruptcy. These include:

- Most taxes (with some exceptions)
- Student loans (unless the debtor can prove undue hardship)
- Child support and alimony payments
- Fines and penalties imposed by government agencies
- Certain types of debts incurred through fraud or misrepresentation
- Debts resulting from a DUI or reckless driving
- Certain types of secured debt, such as a mortgage or car loan, if the debtor wants to keep the property securing the debt

It's important to note that the laws and regulations regarding dischargeable and non-dischargeable debt can vary from state to state, and it's always best to consult with a bankruptcy attorney before filing for Chapter 7 bankruptcy to get a clear understanding of which debts will be dischargeable and which will not.

Certain types of judgments may be dischargeable under Chapter 7 bankruptcy, but it depends on the nature of the judgment and how it was obtained.

- Civil judgments: Civil judgments that result from a lawsuit in which a creditor sues the debtor for unpaid debts, such as credit card debt, medical bills, or personal loans, are generally dischargeable in a Chapter 7 bankruptcy.

- Domestic support obligations: Judgments for domestic support obligations, such as child support and alimony, are not dischargeable in a Chapter 7 bankruptcy.

- Fraudulent judgments: Judgments that result from fraud or misrepresentation, such as a judgment obtained through deceit or misrepresentation, are not dischargeable in a Chapter 7 bankruptcy.

- Criminal judgments: Judgments that result from criminal charges, such as fines or penalties imposed by a court for a criminal conviction, are not dischargeable in a Chapter 7 bankruptcy.

- Certain types of judgments from government agencies: Judgments imposed by government agencies for certain types of violations, such as environmental or securities laws, may not be dischargeable in a Chapter 7 bankruptcy.

It's important to note that the laws and regulations regarding dischargeable and non-dischargeable judgments can vary from state to state, and it's always best to consult with a bankruptcy attorney before filing for Chapter 7 bankruptcy to get a clear understanding of which judgments will be dischargeable and which will not.

Most taxes are not dischargeable in a Chapter 7 bankruptcy, with some exceptions. In general, taxes are considered priority debts, which means that they must be paid before other types of debts.

- Income taxes: Income taxes are generally not dischargeable in a Chapter 7 bankruptcy. However, there are some exceptions. For example, income taxes may be dischargeable if they are more than three years old, were assessed more than 240 days before the bankruptcy filing, and if the debtor did not commit fraud or evade taxes.

- Sales taxes: Sales taxes are not dischargeable in a Chapter 7 bankruptcy.

- Property taxes: Property taxes are not dischargeable in a Chapter 7 bankruptcy if they are less than one year old. However, if the taxes are more than one year old, they may be dischargeable if they are not considered a priority debt.

- Trust Fund Recovery Penalty (TFRP): The Trust Fund Recovery Penalty (TFRP) is a penalty imposed by the IRS on certain individuals who are responsible for collecting, accounting for, and paying over certain employment taxes, like payroll taxes, and fail to do so. TFRP is not dischargeable in a Chapter 7 bankruptcy.

It's important to note that the laws and regulations regarding dischargeable and non-dischargeable taxes can vary from state to state, and it's always best to consult with a bankruptcy attorney or a tax professional before filing for Chapter 7 bankruptcy to get a clear understanding of which taxes will be dischargeable and which will not.

Chapter 13 bankruptcy, also known as "reorganization" bankruptcy, is a type of bankruptcy available to individuals and married couples who have regular income and a significant amount of debt. Unlike Chapter 7 bankruptcy, which liquidates assets to pay off creditors, Chapter 13 bankruptcy allows the debtor to keep their assets and repay their debts over a period of 3 to 5 years through a repayment plan.

When an individual files for Chapter 13 bankruptcy, they must propose a repayment plan that outlines how they will repay their creditors over a 3- to 5-year period. The plan must be approved by the court and the debtor's creditors. The debtor will make payments to the trustee, who will then distribute the payments to the creditors according to the terms of the plan.

One of the main benefits of Chapter 13 bankruptcy is that it allows the debtor to keep their assets, such as their home or car, even if they are behind on payments. The debtor can also use the plan to catch up on missed mortgage or car payments, and pay off certain types of debt that are not dischargeable in a Chapter 7 bankruptcy, such as most taxes or student loans.

The debtor must also attend a meeting of creditors, also known as a "341 meeting," where the trustee and creditors can ask the debtor questions about their financial situation and the proposed repayment plan.

Chapter 13 bankruptcy also provides an automatic stay, which is an order from the court that stops creditors from taking any collection action against the debtor. Once the repayment plan is completed, the debtor will receive a discharge, which releases them from personal liability for most of their dischargeable debts.

It's important to note that the debtor must have a regular income to be eligible for Chapter 13 bankruptcy and the court will consider the debtor's income and expenses when approving a repayment plan. Also, filing for Chapter 13 bankruptcy can have a significant impact on an individual's credit rating, and it will stay in their credit report for up to 7 years.

Part 2: Business Bankruptcy

Chapter 7 business bankruptcy, also known as "liquidation" bankruptcy, is a type of bankruptcy available to businesses that are unable to pay their debts as they become due. The purpose of Chapter 7 business bankruptcy is to sell off the business's assets and use the proceeds to pay off the business's creditors.

When a business files for Chapter 7 bankruptcy, the court will appoint a trustee to oversee the process. The trustee's role is to review the business's assets and determine which assets are exempt and which are non-exempt. Exempt assets are typically those that are necessary for the business's operation, such as equipment and inventory. Non-exempt assets, such as real estate or investments, may be sold by the trustee to pay off the business's creditors.

The business must also submit a list of all their creditors and the amount of money they owe to each one, as well as a schedule of their income and expenses. The business must also attend a meeting of creditors, also known as a "341 meeting," where the trustee and creditors can ask the business questions about their financial situation.

Once the trustee has reviewed the business's assets and determined which assets are non-exempt, the trustee will sell the non-exempt assets and use the proceeds to pay off the business's creditors. Any remaining debt that is not dischargeable will have to be paid by the business.

It's important to note that the Chapter 7 bankruptcy process for businesses is typically quicker than for individuals and can be completed within 3 to 6 months. Also, filing for Chapter 7 bankruptcy will effectively mean the end of the business, and the business's assets will be sold off and the proceeds will be used to pay off the creditors, and the business will be dissolved.

It's also important to note that filing for Chapter 7 bankruptcy can have a significant impact on a business's credit rating and reputation, and it may be difficult for the business to obtain credit or secure loans in the future.

Chapter 11 business bankruptcy, also known as "reorganization" bankruptcy, is a type of bankruptcy available to businesses that wish to continue operating while they reorganize their debts. The purpose of Chapter 11 bankruptcy is to allow the business to restructure its debt and operations in order to become financially viable again.

When a business files for Chapter 11 bankruptcy, it must propose a plan of reorganization to the court. The plan must outline how the business intends to repay its creditors and reorganize its operations. The plan must be approved by the court and the business's creditors. Once the plan is approved, the business will operate under the supervision of the court while it repays its debts according to the terms of the plan.

One of the main benefits of Chapter 11 bankruptcy is that it allows the business to continue operating while it reorganizes its debts. The business can also use the plan to catch up on missed payments, and pay off certain types of debt that are not dischargeable in a Chapter 7 bankruptcy, such as most taxes or certain types of secured debt.

The business must also attend a meeting of creditors, also known as a "341 meeting," where the trustee and creditors can ask the business questions about their financial situation and the proposed plan of reorganization.

Chapter 11 bankruptcy also provides an automatic stay, which is an order from the court that stops creditors from taking any collection action against the business. Once the plan of reorganization is completed, the business will receive a discharge, which releases it from personal liability for most of its dischargeable debts.

It's important to note that the process of Chapter 11 bankruptcy for businesses is more complex and can take longer than for individuals and for Chapter 7. It can take several months to several years to complete the process, and it requires the business to continue operating, which can be difficult in some cases.

Also, the business must have enough income to repay its debts and continue operating, the court will consider the business's income and expenses when approving a plan of reorganization. Filing for Chapter 11 bankruptcy can have a significant impact on a business's credit rating, reputation and future financing, and it's always best to consult with a bankruptcy attorney before filing for Chapter 11 bankruptcy.

Part 3: Defaulting

Defaulting on a loan occurs when a borrower fails to make payments as agreed upon in the loan contract. When a borrower defaults, it can have serious consequences, both for the borrower and for the lender.

For borrowers, defaulting on a loan can damage their credit score and make it more difficult to obtain credit in the future. This can make it harder to get approved for loans, credit cards, and other financial products, and may result in higher interest rates and fees. In addition, borrowers who default on secured loans, such as mortgages or car loans, may risk losing their assets, such as their home or car.

For lenders, defaulting can result in lost revenue and increased costs associated with trying to collect on the debt. In some cases, lenders may take legal action to recover the debt, which can further damage the borrower's credit score and lead to additional fees and penalties.

There are several reasons why a borrower may default on a loan. These can include a sudden change in financial circumstances, such as the loss of a job or a medical emergency, or poor financial management, such as overspending or taking on too much debt. In some cases, borrowers may also default due to fraud or other illegal activity.

If a borrower is struggling to make loan payments, it is important to contact the lender as soon as possible to discuss options for repayment or loan modification. Many lenders are willing to work with borrowers to find a solution that is mutually beneficial and can help avoid default.

Overall, defaulting on a loan can have serious consequences for both borrowers and lenders, and it is important to carefully consider the costs and risks associated with borrowing money before entering into any loan agreement.

Defaulting is a term used to describe a situation in which a borrower fails to make the required payments on a loan or debt. When a borrower defaults, it means they have become delinquent on their payments and have failed to fulfill the terms of their loan agreement. Defaulting on a loan can have serious consequences, including:

1. Damaged credit: Defaulting on a loan can have a significant impact on a person's credit score and remain on their credit report for several years, making it harder for them to obtain credit in the future.

2. Legal action: In some cases, the lender may take legal action to recover the debt, such as filing a lawsuit.

3. Repossession: In the case of defaulting on a secured loan, such as an auto loan or mortgage, the lender may have the right to repossess the collateral used to secure the loan.

4. Garnished wages: If a lender wins a judgment against a borrower in court, they may be able to garnish the borrower's wages to recover the debt.

It's important to make timely payments on all loans and debts to avoid defaulting and the negative consequences that come with it. If a person is struggling to make their loan payments, it may be helpful to reach out to their lender to see if alternative payment arrangements can be made.

Comparing bankruptcy to defaulting

Whether it's better to declare bankruptcy or default on your debts depends on your individual financial situation and the types of debt you have.

Declaring bankruptcy can provide a fresh start for individuals and businesses that are struggling with debt. In a Chapter 7 bankruptcy, for example, many types of unsecured debt can be discharged, allowing you to eliminate those debts and start over. In a Chapter 13 bankruptcy, you can reorganize your debts and repay them over a period of 3 to 5 years through a repayment plan.

Defaulting on your debts, on the other hand, is a failure to repay your debts as agreed, and it can have serious consequences, including:

- Damage to your credit score: Defaulting on your debts can have a significant impact on your credit score and can make it difficult to obtain credit, a loan, or a mortgage in the future.

- Collection actions: If you default on your debts, your creditors may take legal action to collect the debt, including wage garnishment, bank account seizure, and property liens.

- Lawsuits: Your creditors may also file a lawsuit against you in order to collect the debt. If they win the lawsuit, they may be able to obtain a judgment against you, which can lead to wage garnishment, bank account seizure, and other collection actions.

- Lengthy process: Defaulting on your debts can be a lengthy and stressful process, as you'll need to deal with collection actions, lawsuits, and other legal proceedings.

It's always best to consult with a bankruptcy attorney or a financial advisor before making a decision about whether to declare bankruptcy or default on your debts. They can help you understand the benefits and drawbacks of each option and help you determine the best course of action for your specific financial situation.

Part 4: Debt Relief

Debt relief refers to various measures that are taken to help individuals or countries who are unable to repay their debts. These measures can include debt forgiveness, debt restructuring, or a reduction in the amount that is owed. Debt forgiveness involves canceling all or a portion of the debt that is owed, while debt restructuring involves renegotiating the terms of the debt, such as the interest rate or the repayment schedule. Debt relief can also involve a reduction in the amount that is owed, also known as debt reduction. This can be done by writing off a portion of the debt or by extending the repayment period. Debt relief measures can be provided by governments, international organizations, or private creditors and can be intended to help individuals, businesses, or entire countries that are facing financial difficulties.

Debt reduction, also known as debt relief or debt write-off, is a measure in which a lender agrees to reduce the amount of debt that a borrower owes. This can be done by writing off a portion of the debt, or by extending the repayment period.

There are several ways debt reduction can be achieved. One way is through debt forgiveness, in which a lender agrees to forgive a portion of the debt. Another way is through debt restructuring, in which the terms of the debt are renegotiated, such as the interest rate or the repayment schedule. This can make it easier for the borrower to repay the debt.

Debt reduction can be applied to various types of debt, including consumer debt, business debt, and sovereign debt. It can be provided by governments, international organizations, or private creditors and can be intended to help individuals, businesses, or entire countries that are facing financial difficulties.

Like debt forgiveness, debt reduction can have both positive and negative consequences. On one hand, it can provide much-needed relief to individuals and countries facing financial difficulties. On the other hand, it can also create a moral hazard, which is a situation where lenders become more willing to lend money to risky borrowers because they believe that the debt will be reduced if the borrower is unable to repay it. Additionally, debt reduction can also have political and economic implications, particularly in the case of sovereign debt. The decision to reduce debt can be controversial, and it can also have an impact on the country's creditworthiness and the willingness of other creditors to lend to it in the future.

Overall, debt reduction is a measure intended to help individuals, businesses or countries that are facing financial difficulties and are unable to repay their debt. However, it's a measure that needs to be carefully evaluated considering the potential implications.

Debt forgiveness, also known as debt cancellation, is a measure in which a lender agrees to cancel all or a portion of a borrower's debt. This means that the borrower is no longer obligated to repay the forgiven amount. Debt forgiveness can be applied to various types of debt, including consumer debt, business debt, and sovereign debt.

There are several reasons why a lender may choose to forgive debt. For example, in the case of consumer debt, a lender may forgive a portion of the debt to help the borrower avoid bankruptcy or to help the borrower get back on their feet financially. In the case of sovereign debt, a country may be facing a severe economic crisis and may be unable to repay its debts. In this case, international organizations or other creditors may forgive a portion of the country's debt to help it recover.

However, it's important to note that debt forgiveness can have both positive and negative consequences. On one hand, it can provide much-needed relief to individuals and countries facing financial difficulties. On the other hand, it can also create a moral hazard, which is a situation where lenders become more willing to lend money to risky borrowers because they believe that the debt will be forgiven if the borrower is unable to repay it.

Additionally, debt forgiveness can also have political and economic implications, particularly in the case of sovereign debt. The decision to forgive debt can be controversial, and it can also have an impact on the country's creditworthiness and the willingness of other creditors to lend to it in the future.

Yes, there is a type of financial consolidation for individuals, known as debt consolidation. Debt consolidation is a process by which an individual combines multiple outstanding debts, such as credit card debt, personal loans, and medical bills, into a single, new loan with a lower interest rate and/or more favorable terms. The goal of debt consolidation is to make it easier for the individual to manage their debt and pay it off more quickly by reducing the overall cost of the debt and streamlining the repayment process.

There are several ways to consolidate debt, including:

- Taking out a personal loan to pay off other debts: This can be a good option if the individual can qualify for a loan with a lower interest rate than their existing debts.
- Using a balance transfer credit card: This involves transferring multiple credit card balances to a single card with a lower interest rate or promotional rate.
- Enrolling in a debt management plan: This is a repayment plan that is organized by a credit counseling agency and involves consolidating multiple debts into one monthly payment.
- Using a home equity loan or line of credit: This involves borrowing against the equity in an individual's home to pay off other debts.

It's important to note that consolidating debt doesn't make the debt disappear, it just changes the form it takes and can make it more manageable. Also, depending on the method of consolidation, you may be taking on a secured debt in place of unsecured debt, which can have different implications on your credit score and assets. It's recommended to consult a financial advisor or credit counselor before making any decision.

Chapter 3: Credit

Credit refers to the ability of a borrower to obtain goods or services before payment, based on the promise to pay later. Credit can come in various forms, including loans, credit cards, lines of credit, and mortgages.

Credit is important because it allows individuals and businesses to make purchases and investments that they otherwise could not afford. However, credit also comes with risks, such as the possibility of defaulting on payments and accruing interest charges.

To obtain credit, borrowers must demonstrate creditworthiness by showing that they have a reliable income and a good credit history. Credit scores, which are based on credit history and other factors, are used by lenders to assess a borrower's creditworthiness.

When using credit, borrowers must make timely payments to avoid late fees and damage to their credit scores. Interest rates also apply to credit, meaning that borrowers will have to pay back more than the amount they borrowed.

Overall, credit can be a useful financial tool, but it's important to use it responsibly and understand the terms and conditions of the credit agreement.

Part 1: Credit Building

Building credit is a process of establishing a positive credit history that demonstrates to lenders that you are a responsible borrower. Here are some steps you can take to build your credit:

1. Get a credit card: Obtaining a credit card and using it responsibly is one of the easiest ways to start building credit. Make sure to use it regularly and pay the balance in full each month.

2. Make payments on time: Late payments have a negative impact on your credit score, so it's important to make all of your payments on time.

3. Keep credit card balances low: High credit card balances can indicate that you are overextended and may have trouble repaying your debt. Keeping your balances low relative to your credit limits shows lenders that you are a responsible borrower.

4. Apply for credit only as needed: Every time you apply for credit, it results in a hard inquiry on your credit report, which can temporarily lower your credit score. So, it's important to only apply for credit when you need it.

5. Diversify your credit: A mix of different types of credit, such as a credit card, auto loan, and mortgage, can help build your credit.

6. Monitor your credit report: Regularly monitoring your credit report can help you spot errors and potential fraud, and give you the opportunity to dispute any inaccuracies.

Building credit takes time, but with persistence and responsible financial habits, you can establish a positive credit history and improve your credit score.

There are several factors that can damage a person's credit, including:

1. Late payments: Late payments can have a significant impact on a person's credit score, especially if they are habitually late.

2. High credit card balances: Maintaining high credit card balances relative to the credit limit can indicate to lenders that a person may be overextended and may have trouble repaying their debts.

3. Maxing out credit cards: Maxing out credit cards can have a negative impact on a person's credit utilization ratio, which is a key factor in determining their credit score.

4. Applying for too much credit at once: Every time a person applies for credit, it results in a hard inquiry on their credit report, which can temporarily lower their credit score.

5. Defaulting on a loan: Defaulting on a loan, such as a mortgage or auto loan, can have a significant impact on a person's credit score and remain on their credit report for several years.

6. Debt collections: Debt collections, especially those that go to court, can also have a negative impact on a person's credit score and remain on their credit report for several years.

7. Bankruptcy: Filing for bankruptcy can have a major impact on a person's credit score and remain on their credit report for up to 10 years.

It's important to be aware of these factors and to take steps to maintain a positive credit history and improve your credit score. This includes making payments on time, keeping credit card balances low, and monitoring your credit report regularly.

Part 2: Credit Card

You can apply for a credit card from most major banks, credit unions, and other financial institutions. You can also apply for a credit card online, through the mail, or by phone.

When to apply for a credit card:

- You may want to consider applying for a credit card when you need to make a large purchase and want to spread the payments out over time.
- If you're planning to travel and want to use a credit card to book flights, hotels, and rental cars.
- If you want to build or improve your credit score.

Where to apply for a credit card:

- Banks: Most banks offer credit cards. You can check with the bank where you have your checking or savings account.
- Credit card companies: Many credit card companies, such as Visa, Mastercard, Discover, and American Express, have their own credit cards.
- Online: There are many websites that allow you to compare credit card offers and apply for a credit card online.
- Credit unions: Some credit unions also offer credit cards to their members.

When applying for a credit card, it's important to compare different offers and choose the one that best meets your needs. You can also check your credit score and financial history before applying to increase your chances of being approved.

There are several reasons why an individual may be denied a credit card. Some common reasons include:

1. Insufficient credit history: If an individual has little or no credit history, they may be denied a credit card because lenders view them as a higher risk.

2. Poor credit score: If an individual has a low credit score, they may be denied a credit card because lenders view them as a higher risk.
3. High debt-to-income ratio: If an individual has a high level of existing debt relative to their income, they may be denied a credit card because lenders view them as a higher risk.
4. Unverifiable income: If an individual is unable to provide proof of income, they may be denied a credit card because lenders view them as a higher risk.
5. Fraud or identity theft: If an individual's credit history has been impacted by fraud or identity theft, they may be denied a credit card.

Pitfalls of having a credit card:

1. High-interest rates: Credit cards often have high-interest rates, which can make it difficult to pay off balances if you carry them over from month to month.
2. Fees: Some credit cards charge annual fees, balance transfer fees, and other types of fees, which can add up over time.
3. Temptation to overspend: Credit cards can make it easy to overspend, which can lead to high levels of debt.
4. It can impact your credit score: If you miss payments, have high balances, or max out your credit card, it can negatively impact your credit score.
5. It can be harder to budget: Credit cards can make it harder to stick to a budget because it's easy to lose track of how much you're spending.

It's important to be aware of these potential pitfalls and use credit cards responsibly. It's also a good idea to review your credit report periodically and take steps to improve your credit score if necessary.

A high debt-to-income (DTI) ratio can make it difficult to get approved for a credit card or other types of credit. Here are some steps you can take to lower your DTI ratio and improve your chances of getting approved for a credit card:

1. Pay off existing debts: Focus on paying off high-interest credit card balances or other types of debt first. This can help lower your DTI ratio and improve your credit score.
2. Increase your income: You can work on increasing your income by getting a higher paying job, starting a side hustle or business, or finding other ways to earn more money.
3. Create a budget: Create a budget that allows you to live within your means and prioritize paying off debt. This will help you gain control over your spending and improve your DTI ratio.
4. Limit new credit applications: Every time you apply for credit, a hard inquiry is made on your credit report, which can lower your credit score. limit the number of new credit applications you make.
5. Consider a debt consolidation loan: If you have multiple high-interest debts, a debt consolidation loan can help you pay them off at a lower interest rate and with one monthly payment.
6. Seek credit counseling: If you are having trouble managing your debt, consider seeking credit counseling from a non-profit organization. They can help you create a plan to pay off your debts and improve your credit.

It's important to remember that improving your DTI ratio and credit score takes time and effort, but with persistence and a plan, you can achieve your goals and be approved for a credit card.

Part 3: Credit Reporting

A credit report is a detailed record of an individual's credit history, including information about their credit accounts, payment history, and other financial activities. Credit reports are compiled by credit reporting agencies, which gather information from various sources, including banks, credit card companies, and other lenders.

Credit reports typically include information such as the individual's name, address, date of birth, and Social Security number. They also include a list of all the credit accounts that the individual has, along with information about the account balances, payment history, and credit limits.

In addition to credit accounts, credit reports may also include information about other financial activities, such as bankruptcies, foreclosures, and collections. They may also include inquiries, which are records of any time someone has requested a copy of the individual's credit report.

Credit reports are used by lenders, landlords, employers, and other organizations to evaluate an individual's creditworthiness and ability to manage debt. A good credit report can make it easier to obtain loans, credit cards, and other financial products at favorable interest rates, while a poor credit report can make it more difficult and expensive to obtain credit.

Under U.S. law, individuals are entitled to a free copy of their credit report from each of the three major credit reporting agencies (Equifax, Experian, and TransUnion) once every 12 months. It's a good idea to review your credit report regularly to make sure it's accurate and up-to-date, and to address any errors or discrepancies that may be affecting your credit score.

A credit report typically contains a wide range of information about an individual's credit history and financial behavior. Some of the key items that are included in a credit report are:

1. Personal information: This includes the person's name, current and previous addresses, Social Security number, and date of birth.

2. Credit accounts: This section lists all of the credit accounts that the person has opened, such as credit cards, loans, and mortgages. Each account includes information such as the creditor's name, account number, date opened, credit limit or loan amount, and payment history.

3. Payment history: This section shows the person's payment history for each of their credit accounts. It includes information on whether payments were made on time, late, or missed altogether, and how long overdue payments were.

4. Collections and public records: This section lists any collections, bankruptcies, foreclosures, or other public records related to the person's credit history.

5. Credit inquiries: This section shows any recent inquiries made by lenders or other parties who have requested a copy of the person's credit report.

6. Credit score: The credit report may also include the person's credit score, which is a numerical representation of their creditworthiness based on the information in the report.

Overall, a credit report provides a detailed snapshot of a person's credit history and financial behavior, which lenders and other parties use to evaluate their creditworthiness and ability to repay debts.

Credit reports are used by a variety of entities, including lenders, credit card issuers, landlords, employers, and insurance companies, to assess an individual's creditworthiness and financial history. Here are some specific uses of a credit report:

1. Lending decisions: Banks, credit unions, and other lenders use credit reports to determine whether to approve an individual's

loan application, and if so, what interest rate to charge. A person's credit score and credit history are important factors in these decisions.

2. Credit card applications: Credit card companies use credit reports to assess an individual's creditworthiness and determine whether to approve their application for a credit card. A person's credit score and credit history are key factors in these decisions.

3. Rental applications: Landlords often use credit reports to evaluate potential tenants, especially in competitive rental markets. A person's credit history can indicate their ability to pay rent on time and be a responsible tenant.

4. Employment decisions: Employers may use credit reports as part of the hiring process, especially for jobs that require financial responsibility or access to sensitive financial information. In some states, employers are required to get a person's permission before accessing their credit report.

5. Insurance applications: Insurance companies may use credit reports to help determine premiums and rates for policies, as credit history can be an indicator of risk.

6. Identity verification: Credit reports can also be used to verify a person's identity, as they contain sensitive personal information such as name, address, and Social Security number.

Overall, credit reports play a crucial role in many important financial and personal decisions, and it's important for individuals to regularly check their credit report for accuracy and take steps to improve their credit if necessary.

Not having a credit report can be a disadvantage for individuals who are trying to establish creditworthiness and access credit products. Here are some potential pitfalls of not having a credit report:

1. Difficulty getting approved for credit: Without a credit report, lenders may not have enough information to assess an individual's creditworthiness and may be less likely to approve their loan or credit card application. This can make it difficult to access credit products, such as a mortgage or car loan.

2. Higher interest rates and fees: If an individual is approved for credit without a credit report, they may be charged higher interest rates or fees because lenders consider them to be a higher risk borrower.

3. Limited access to certain services: Some services, such as renting an apartment or getting a cell phone contract, may require a credit check as part of the application process. Without a credit report, an individual may have limited options or be required to pay a deposit.

4. Missed opportunities to build credit: Without a credit report, individuals may miss out on opportunities to build credit, such as by using a credit card responsibly or making on-time payments on a loan.

5. Increased vulnerability to identity theft: Without a credit report, individuals may not be aware of fraudulent activity on their credit accounts and could be at increased risk of identity theft.

Overall, not having a credit report can make it difficult for individuals to access credit products, build credit, and take advantage of certain services. It's important for individuals to establish credit early and monitor their credit report regularly to avoid these potential pitfalls.

Part 4: Credit Repair

Credit repair is the process of improving a person's credit standing by identifying and correcting errors on their credit report and negotiating with creditors to have negative items removed. The goal is to increase the individual's credit score, making it easier for them to obtain loans, credit cards, and other financial products with better terms and lower interest rates. Some common methods of credit repair include disputing errors on credit reports, paying off debt, and creating a budget to manage finances effectively. It's important to note that while credit repair can be a helpful tool, there are no guarantees and some credit repair services may use unethical or even illegal methods to improve a person's credit score.

Some credit repair services may use unethical or even illegal methods to improve a person's credit score, such as fabricating information on credit reports, creating false identities, or disputing legitimate negative items without proper cause. It's important to be cautious when choosing a credit repair service and to research their reputation and methods before signing up. Consumers should also be aware that they have the right to dispute errors on their own credit reports and to repair their credit on their own, without paying for a credit repair service.

Credit repair refers to the process of improving one's creditworthiness, which is determined by their credit score. Credit scores are calculated based on various factors such as payment history, amounts owed, length of credit history, types of credit used, and new credit.

If an individual's credit score is low, they may face difficulty in getting approved for loans or credit cards, and may also be required to pay higher interest rates. In order to improve their credit score, they may engage in credit repair strategies.

The first step in credit repair is to obtain a copy of one's credit report from one or more of the credit bureaus. This report will provide information about an individual's credit history, including any negative items that may be bringing down their score. It is important to review the report carefully to ensure that all information is accurate and up-to-date.

If there are any errors or inaccuracies, they should be disputed with the credit bureau.

Next, an individual may work to pay off outstanding debts, particularly those that are in collections or past due. This can help to improve their payment history and reduce their overall debt-to-income ratio, both of which can positively impact their credit score.

Additionally, an individual may consider opening new credit accounts, such as a secured credit card or a credit builder loan, in order to demonstrate responsible credit behavior and increase their credit utilization ratio. However, it is important to use these accounts responsibly and to avoid accruing too much debt.

Finally, an individual may also consider working with a credit counseling agency or a credit repair company. These organizations can provide guidance and support in improving one's credit score, but it is important to research and choose a reputable organization to avoid scams or fraudulent practices.

Overall, credit repair involves a combination of strategies to improve one's creditworthiness and demonstrate responsible credit behavior. It may take time and effort, but improving one's credit score can have a positive impact on their financial future.

Secured credit cards are often considered the best type of credit card to help with credit repair. With a secured credit card, the cardholder is required to make a deposit, which becomes the card's credit limit. This means that the credit card company has collateral in case the cardholder is unable to pay their balance.

Using a secured credit card responsibly and making on-time payments can help improve an individual's credit score over time. This is because the credit card company will report the individual's payment history to the credit bureaus, which can demonstrate responsible credit behavior and help to increase their credit score.

Another option for credit repair is to look for credit cards designed specifically for individuals with low or fair credit scores. These cards may have higher interest rates or annual fees, but they can provide an opportunity to demonstrate responsible credit behavior and build a positive credit history.

It is important to research and compare different credit cards to find the best option for individual needs and financial situations. It is also important to use credit cards responsibly, paying balances in full and on time, and avoiding accruing too much debt.

Chapter 4: Insurance

Insurance is a contractual arrangement in which an individual or an entity (such as a business) pays a premium to an insurance company in exchange for protection against financial losses or damages that may arise due to unexpected events. These events can include accidents, illnesses, theft, natural disasters, or other risks that may affect the insured.

The insurance company pools the premiums it receives from its policyholders and uses them to pay for any losses or damages incurred by its insured clients. The terms of an insurance policy typically specify the types of events that are covered, the amount of coverage provided, and the conditions under which claims can be made.

There are many types of insurance policies available, such as health insurance, auto insurance, homeowner's insurance, life insurance, disability insurance, and business insurance. Each type of insurance policy provides a different kind of protection, and the terms and coverage may vary widely depending on the insurance company and the individual policy.

In summary, insurance is a risk management tool that helps individuals and businesses protect themselves against unexpected financial losses by transferring the risk to an insurance company in exchange for a premium.

Insurance provides several benefits to individuals, businesses, and society as a whole. Here are some of the key benefits of insurance:

1. Financial Protection: Insurance provides financial protection against unexpected events, such as accidents, illnesses, natural disasters, or lawsuits. Insurance can help cover the costs of medical expenses, property damage, or legal fees, protecting individuals and businesses from significant financial losses.

2. Risk Management: Insurance helps individuals and businesses manage risk by transferring some of the financial risks associated with unexpected events to an insurance company. This allows individuals and businesses to focus on their core activities without worrying about the financial consequences of unexpected events.

3. Peace of Mind: Knowing that they are protected against unexpected events can provide individuals and businesses with peace of mind, reducing stress and anxiety.

4. Social Responsibility: Insurance promotes social responsibility by encouraging individuals and businesses to take measures to prevent or minimize the risks associated with unexpected events. For example, a business may install safety equipment to reduce the risk of accidents, or an individual may take steps to maintain their health to reduce the risk of illness.

5. Economic Stability: Insurance helps promote economic stability by providing a safety net for individuals and businesses. Without insurance, unexpected events could lead to significant financial losses and economic instability.

Overall, insurance plays a critical role in promoting financial stability, risk management, and social responsibility, providing individuals, businesses, and society as a whole with important benefits.

Not having insurance can leave individuals and businesses vulnerable to financial losses and other negative consequences. Here are some of the pitfalls of not having insurance:

1. Financial risk: Without insurance, individuals or businesses are responsible for paying all costs associated with unexpected events such as accidents, illnesses, or natural disasters. This can lead to

significant financial burdens, including debt, bankruptcy, or loss of assets.

2. Legal risk: If an individual or business is found liable for damages or injuries resulting from an accident or other event, they may be required to pay costly legal fees and settlements. Without liability insurance, these expenses can be significant and may result in financial ruin.

3. Health risk: Without health insurance, individuals may be unable to afford necessary medical care, which can lead to delayed treatment, worsening health conditions, or even death.

4. Professional risk: Professionals such as doctors, lawyers, and accountants may face significant risks if they do not carry professional liability insurance. Without this coverage, they may be exposed to financial losses resulting from lawsuits or other legal claims against them.

5. Reduced access to credit: Lenders may be less likely to approve loans or lines of credit for individuals or businesses that do not have insurance, as they are seen as higher risk borrowers.

In summary, not having insurance can leave individuals and businesses vulnerable to significant financial, legal, and health risks. It's important to carefully consider the potential consequences of not having insurance and to choose policies that provide adequate protection against these risks.

If you ever want to file an insurance claim, the following documents may be required:

1. Insurance policy: A copy of your insurance policy, which outlines the coverage and terms of your insurance plan.

2. Claim form: A form provided by your insurance company that you must fill out to initiate the claim process.

3. Proof of loss: Documentation that verifies the damage or loss you are claiming, such as photographs, videos, or witness statements.

4. Police report: A report from law enforcement, if applicable, such as in the case of theft or vandalism.

5. Medical records: If the claim is related to a medical issue, medical records and bills may be required.

6. Repair estimates: If the claim is related to damage to property, such as a car or home, repair estimates from reputable repair shops may be required.

7. Receipts: Receipts for items that were damaged or stolen, if applicable.

8. Any other relevant documentation: Any other documentation that may be relevant to your claim, such as invoices or contracts.

It's important to note that the specific documents required may vary depending on the type of insurance policy and the nature of the claim. It's always a good idea to check with your insurance company in advance to confirm their requirements.

Part 1: Types of Insurance

There are many types of insurance available to individuals and businesses, each providing protection against different types of risks. Some of the most common types of insurance include:

1. Health Insurance: Health insurance policies cover the cost of medical expenses, including doctor's visits, hospital stays, prescription drugs, and medical procedures.

2. Life Insurance: Life insurance policies provide financial protection to the family or dependents of the policyholder in the event of the policyholder's death.

3. Auto Insurance: Auto insurance policies provide coverage for damages or injuries that result from accidents involving automobiles, trucks, or other vehicles.

4. Homeowner's Insurance: Homeowner's insurance policies provide coverage for damages or losses to a home or its contents caused by events such as fire, theft, or natural disasters.

5. Disability Insurance: Disability insurance policies provide income replacement in the event that the policyholder becomes disabled and is unable to work.

6. Travel Insurance: Travel insurance policies provide coverage for unexpected events that may occur while traveling, such as medical emergencies, trip cancellations, or lost luggage.

7. Liability Insurance: Liability insurance policies protect individuals or businesses against financial losses that may arise from legal claims or lawsuits.

8. Business Insurance: Business insurance policies provide coverage for a variety of risks that may affect a business, including property damage, liability claims, and business interruption.

These are just a few examples of the many types of insurance available. It's important to carefully consider the risks that may affect you or your business and to choose insurance policies that provide adequate protection against those risks.

Health Insurance

Health insurance is a type of insurance that provides financial protection against medical expenses and healthcare costs. Health insurance policies typically cover a range of medical services, including doctor's visits, hospital stays, prescription drugs, medical procedures, and diagnostic tests.

There are several types of health insurance plans, including:

1. Employer-Sponsored Health Insurance: Many employers offer health insurance plans to their employees as part of their benefits package. These plans may cover the employee, their spouse, and their children.

2. Individual Health Insurance: Individuals can purchase health insurance plans directly from insurance companies or through government-run health insurance marketplaces.

3. Medicare: Medicare is a government-run health insurance program that provides coverage to people who are 65 years or older, as well as those with certain disabilities.

4. Medicaid: Medicaid is a government-run health insurance program that provides coverage to low-income individuals and families.

The cost of health insurance premiums can vary widely depending on the plan, the level of coverage, and the age and health of the insured person. Some health insurance plans require deductibles, which is the amount of money the insured person must pay before their insurance coverage begins.

In addition to premiums and deductibles, health insurance plans may also have co-payments, which are the out-of-pocket expenses that the insured person is responsible for paying at the time of a medical service. Some plans may also have coinsurance, which is the percentage of the medical costs that the insured person is responsible for paying after the deductible has been met.

It's important to carefully review the terms and coverage of health insurance policies to ensure that they provide adequate protection against unexpected medical expenses.

Life Insurance

Life insurance is a type of insurance policy that provides financial protection to the beneficiaries of the policy in the event of the policyholder's death. The beneficiaries can be any person or entity named in the policy, such as a spouse, child, business partner, or charity.

There are two main types of life insurance: term life insurance and permanent life insurance.

1. Term Life Insurance: Term life insurance provides coverage for a specific period of time, such as 10, 20, or 30 years. The policy pays out a death benefit if the insured person dies during the term of the policy. Term life insurance policies typically have lower premiums than permanent life insurance policies.

2. Permanent Life Insurance: Permanent life insurance provides coverage for the insured person's entire lifetime, as long as the premiums are paid. Permanent life insurance policies can have a

savings component, which builds cash value over time. These policies can also provide an option to borrow against the cash value or withdraw it as needed. Permanent life insurance policies have higher premiums than term life insurance policies.

The cost of life insurance premiums can vary depending on several factors, including the policyholder's age, health, and lifestyle habits, as well as the type and amount of coverage desired.

Life insurance policies can provide a range of benefits, including:

1. Income Replacement: Life insurance can provide financial support to the policyholder's family or dependents in the event of the policyholder's death. This can help replace lost income and cover expenses such as mortgage payments, education costs, and daily living expenses.
2. Estate Planning: Life insurance can be used as a tool for estate planning, providing funds to pay estate taxes and other costs associated with transferring assets to beneficiaries.
3. Business Succession Planning: Life insurance can be used to fund buy-sell agreements for business owners, providing a way to transfer ownership of a business in the event of an owner's death.

It's important to carefully consider the type and amount of life insurance coverage needed to provide adequate financial protection for the policyholder's beneficiaries.

Auto Insurance

Auto insurance is a type of insurance policy that provides financial protection against damages or injuries resulting from a car accident. Auto insurance policies can also provide coverage for theft, vandalism, and other types of damage to a vehicle.

There are several types of auto insurance coverage, including:

1. Liability Coverage: Liability coverage is required by law in most states and provides protection if the policyholder is found to be at fault in an accident that causes damage or injury to another person or their property.

2. Collision Coverage: Collision coverage provides protection for damages to the policyholder's vehicle resulting from a collision with another vehicle or object, regardless of who is at fault.

3. Comprehensive Coverage: Comprehensive coverage provides protection for damages to the policyholder's vehicle resulting from non-collision events, such as theft, vandalism, or natural disasters.

4. Personal Injury Protection (PIP): PIP coverage provides coverage for medical expenses and lost wages resulting from injuries sustained in an auto accident, regardless of who is at fault.

5. Uninsured/Underinsured Motorist Coverage: Uninsured/underinsured motorist coverage provides protection if the policyholder is involved in an accident with a driver who does not have insurance or does not have enough insurance to cover the damages.

The cost of auto insurance premiums can vary depending on several factors, including the policyholder's age, gender, driving history, location, and the type and value of the vehicle being insured.

It's important to carefully review the terms and coverage of auto insurance policies to ensure that they provide adequate protection against unexpected damages or injuries resulting from car accidents. Many states require drivers to carry a minimum amount of liability coverage, but it may be necessary to purchase additional coverage depending on the level of risk and the value of the vehicle being insured.

Automobile Accidents

Automobile accidents can have a range of negative impacts, both for individuals involved in the accident and for society as a whole. Some of the potential pitfalls of an automobile accident include:

1. Physical injuries: Accidents can result in serious physical injuries, such as broken bones, head injuries, and even fatalities.

2. Psychological trauma: Accidents can also cause psychological trauma, such as anxiety, depression, and post-traumatic stress disorder (PTSD).

3. Financial costs: Accidents can be expensive, with costs for medical treatment, repairs to vehicles, and legal expenses.

4. Lost income: Individuals involved in accidents may be unable to work, resulting in lost income and financial stress.

5. Increased insurance premiums: Accidents can result in higher insurance premiums, which can be a significant financial burden.

6. Legal implications: Accidents can result in legal proceedings, such as lawsuits, which can be time-consuming and stressful.

7. Social impact: Accidents can also have a wider social impact, as they may disrupt traffic, cause delays, and result in road closures.

Overall, automobile accidents can have serious and far-reaching consequences, making it important to take measures to prevent them from happening.

Automobile accidents can be very costly, with a range of financial expenses that can add up quickly. Some of the financial costs of an automobile accident include:

1. Medical expenses: If individuals are injured in an accident, they
    may require medical treatment, including emergency room visits,
    hospital stays, and rehabilitation. These expenses can be
    substantial, especially if they require long-term care.
2. Vehicle repairs: Vehicles involved in accidents will likely require
    repairs, which can be costly, depending on the extent of the
    damage.
3. Insurance costs: Accidents can result in higher insurance
    premiums, and individuals may also be responsible for
    deductibles and co-payments.
4. Legal expenses: If an accident results in legal proceedings, such
    as a lawsuit, individuals may incur significant legal expenses,
    including court costs, attorney's fees, and settlement costs.
5. Lost income: If individuals are unable to work as a result of an
    accident, they may experience lost income and financial stress.
6. Decreased property value: If a vehicle is involved in an accident
    and is repaired, its value may be decreased, resulting in a financial
    loss.

Overall, the financial costs of an automobile accident can be substantial,
and it's important for individuals to consider these potential costs when
making decisions about driving, insurance, and safety.

Certain locations can be more prone to automobile accidents for various
reasons, including:

1. Urban areas: Urban areas often have higher traffic volume and
    more congestion, which can increase the risk of accidents.

2. Highways and interstates: Highways and interstates can be more dangerous than other roads due to high speeds and limited visibility.

3. Rural roads: Rural roads may be more prone to accidents due to factors such as narrow lanes, curves, and limited visibility.

4. Construction zones: Construction zones often have lane closures, detours, and other changes to the normal traffic flow that can increase the risk of accidents.

5. School zones: School zones are often busy during drop-off and pick-up times, with a higher volume of children and pedestrians, which can increase the risk of accidents.

6. Areas with poor road conditions: Roads that are in poor condition, such as those with potholes or limited signage, can be more dangerous and prone to accidents.

It's important to be aware of these and other factors when driving, and to adjust your driving accordingly to minimize the risk of accidents. Safe driving practices, such as obeying traffic laws, avoiding distractions, and staying alert, are also critical in reducing the risk of accidents, no matter where you are driving.

Automobile Safety

Automobile safety refers to measures and technologies designed to prevent or reduce the severity of injuries in the event of a car crash. Here are a few key elements of automobile safety:

1. Vehicle design: Vehicle design plays a critical role in automobile safety. Modern vehicles are engineered to reduce the risk of injury during a crash, with features like reinforced structures, crumple zones, and airbags.

2. Seat belts: Seat belts are one of the most effective ways to prevent injuries in the event of an accident. They help to keep individuals in place and reduce the risk of serious injury or death.

3. Child safety seats: Child safety seats are designed to protect children during car trips. They are typically required by law for children under a certain age or weight.

4. Airbags: Airbags are designed to protect individuals during a crash, by deploying in a way that helps to absorb the force of impact.

5. Electronic stability control (ESC): ESC is a technology that helps drivers maintain control of their vehicles during sudden maneuvers, such as swerving to avoid a collision.

6. Advanced driver-assistance systems (ADAS): ADAS are technologies that help drivers avoid accidents, such as lane departure warning systems, blind-spot detection, and automatic emergency braking.

7. Safe driving practices: Safe driving practices, such as obeying traffic laws, avoiding distractions, and wearing seat belts, are essential for reducing the risk of accidents.

Overall, automobile safety is a complex and multi-faceted field, encompassing everything from vehicle design to individual driving habits. By taking a comprehensive approach to automobile safety, we can reduce the number and severity of accidents on our roads.

Safe driving habits are behaviors and actions that can help to reduce the risk of automobile accidents and injuries. Here are a few examples of safe driving habits:

1. Obey traffic laws: Following traffic laws, such as speed limits and stop signs, is critical for maintaining safe and orderly roadways.

2. Avoid distractions: Distracted driving is a major cause of accidents. To avoid distractions, drivers should avoid activities such as texting, eating, or using a GPS while driving.

3. Wear seat belts: Seat belts are one of the most effective ways to prevent injuries in the event of an accident. It's important to wear them at all times when driving or riding in a vehicle.

4. Maintain a safe following distance: Maintaining a safe following distance behind the vehicle in front of you can give you more time to react in the event of an unexpected stop.

5. Stay alert and well-rested: Driving while drowsy or fatigued can be extremely dangerous. Drivers should get plenty of rest before driving and avoid driving when they feel sleepy.

6. Avoid aggressive driving: Aggressive driving, such as tailgating, cutting off other drivers, and excessive speeding, can increase the risk of accidents.

7. Stay focused: Avoid distractions such as playing with the radio or talking to passengers. Stay focused on the road and your surroundings to ensure a safe and enjoyable trip.

8. Adjust your driving to weather and road conditions: Adverse weather conditions, such as rain, snow, and fog, can make driving more challenging. It's important to adjust your driving to match the conditions, such as slowing down and increasing your following distance.

By following safe driving habits, individuals can help to reduce the risk of accidents and maintain a safe and enjoyable driving experience.

Reliability of a car can vary greatly depending on various factors such as the make, model, and year of the vehicle, as well as the driving habits and maintenance of the owner. That being said, here are some car brands and types that are generally known for their reliability:

1. Japanese car brands: Japanese car brands such as Honda, Toyota, and Mazda are known for their reliability and durability.

2. German car brands: German car brands such as Mercedes-Benz, BMW, and Audi are also known for their reliability, although they may have a higher cost of ownership due to their luxury features.

3. Electric and hybrid vehicles: Electric and hybrid vehicles, such as the Tesla Model 3 and Toyota Prius, have relatively few moving parts and can be more reliable than traditional gasoline-powered vehicles.

4. Subaru: Subaru is a well-regarded brand known for its all-wheel drive vehicles, which can be reliable in a variety of weather conditions.

5. Kia and Hyundai: Kia and Hyundai have improved their reliability over the past several years and now offer a variety of vehicles with good reputations for durability and longevity.

It's important to note that reliability is not always a guarantee and can be influenced by various factors such as maintenance and usage. Before purchasing a vehicle, it's recommended to research the make and model, read reviews, and consider getting a pre-purchase inspection to assess its overall condition.

Homeowner's Insurance

Homeowner's insurance is a type of insurance policy that provides financial protection to homeowners against damages or losses to their home and personal property. Homeowner's insurance policies typically cover a range of perils, including damage caused by fire, theft, vandalism, and weather-related events such as hurricanes, tornadoes, and hailstorms.

There are several types of coverage included in a standard homeowner's insurance policy, including:

1. Dwelling Coverage: Dwelling coverage provides protection for the structure of the home, including the foundation, walls, roof, and other attached structures, such as garages or sheds.

2. Personal Property Coverage: Personal property coverage provides protection for the policyholder's personal belongings, such as furniture, clothing, and electronics.

3. Liability Coverage: Liability coverage provides protection if someone is injured on the policyholder's property or if the policyholder causes damage to someone else's property.

4. Additional Living Expenses Coverage: Additional living expenses coverage provides coverage for expenses incurred if the policyholder's home is damaged and they are temporarily displaced, such as hotel costs or rental expenses.

The cost of homeowner's insurance premiums can vary depending on several factors, including the location and value of the home, the level of coverage desired, and the policyholder's claims history.

It's important to carefully review the terms and coverage of homeowner's insurance policies to ensure that they provide adequate protection against unexpected damages or losses to the home and personal property. It may be necessary to purchase additional coverage depending on the level of risk and the value of the home and personal belongings.

Travel Insurance

Travel insurance is a type of insurance policy that provides financial protection against unexpected events that may occur while traveling. Travel insurance can provide coverage for a variety of situations, including medical emergencies, trip cancellation or interruption, lost or stolen luggage, and travel-related accidents.

There are several types of coverage included in a travel insurance policy, including:

1. Trip Cancellation/Interruption Coverage: Trip cancellation/interruption coverage provides protection if the policyholder has to cancel or cut short their trip due to unexpected events, such as illness or injury, natural disasters, or airline strikes.

2. Medical Coverage: Medical coverage provides protection for medical emergencies that occur while traveling, including emergency medical and dental care, hospitalization, and medical evacuation.

3. Evacuation Coverage: Evacuation coverage provides protection if the policyholder needs to be evacuated from a remote or dangerous location due to injury or illness.

4. Baggage Coverage: Baggage coverage provides protection for lost, stolen, or damaged baggage, as well as reimbursement for necessary items if baggage is delayed.

5. Accidental Death and Dismemberment Coverage: Accidental death and dismemberment coverage provides protection for injuries or death resulting from travel-related accidents.

The cost of travel insurance premiums can vary depending on several factors, including the level of coverage desired, the length and destination of the trip, and the policyholder's age and health.

It's important to carefully review the terms and coverage of travel insurance policies to ensure that they provide adequate protection against unexpected events that may occur while traveling. It may be necessary to purchase additional coverage depending on the level of risk and the type of travel activities planned.

Liability Insurance

Liability insurance is a type of insurance policy that provides financial protection against legal claims and expenses resulting from injuries or damages caused by the policyholder. Liability insurance can provide coverage for a variety of situations, including accidents, injuries, property damage, and lawsuits.

There are several types of liability insurance coverage, including:

1. General Liability Insurance: General liability insurance provides protection for businesses against claims of bodily injury, property damage, and advertising injury. This type of coverage is typically required for businesses that operate in public spaces or interact with customers.

2. Professional Liability Insurance: Professional liability insurance, also known as errors and omissions insurance, provides protection for professionals against claims of negligence or malpractice.

3. Product Liability Insurance: Product liability insurance provides protection for businesses against claims of injury or damages caused by products they manufacture or sell.

4. Umbrella Liability Insurance: Umbrella liability insurance provides additional coverage above and beyond the limits of other

liability insurance policies. This type of coverage can help protect against large lawsuits or catastrophic events.

The cost of liability insurance premiums can vary depending on several factors, including the level of coverage desired, the type of business or profession, and the risk level associated with the policyholder's activities.

It's important to carefully review the terms and coverage of liability insurance policies to ensure that they provide adequate protection against unexpected legal claims and expenses. It may be necessary to purchase additional coverage depending on the level of risk and the type of activities or products involved.

Part 2: Healthcare

Healthcare refers to the maintenance or improvement of one's physical, mental, and emotional well-being. It encompasses a broad range of activities, services, and professionals aimed at preventing, diagnosing, treating, and managing illnesses, injuries, and other health-related conditions.

Healthcare includes a variety of services and facilities, including hospitals, clinics, medical laboratories, pharmacies, and rehabilitation centers, among others. Healthcare professionals are also essential components of the healthcare system, and they play various roles depending on their specialty and training. Examples of healthcare professionals include doctors, nurses, pharmacists, physical therapists, and occupational therapists, among others.

The healthcare system also includes various medical technologies, equipment, and procedures used to diagnose and treat health conditions, such as X-rays, MRI scans, surgical procedures, and prescription medications.

Overall, healthcare is a complex and multifaceted field that involves the collaboration of various stakeholders, including healthcare providers, patients, policymakers, insurers, and researchers, among others, to ensure the best possible outcomes for individuals and communities' health.

While healthcare is essential for maintaining good health and treating illnesses, there are also some pitfalls associated with needing healthcare. Some of these pitfalls include:

1. Cost: One of the biggest challenges associated with healthcare is the cost. Healthcare can be very expensive, and many people may not be able to afford the care they need. This can lead to people delaying or avoiding necessary medical treatment, which can

worsen their condition and lead to more significant health problems.

2. Access: Even if people can afford healthcare, they may not have access to it. This can be due to factors such as geographic location, lack of insurance coverage, or a shortage of healthcare providers in their area. Lack of access to healthcare can lead to delayed diagnosis and treatment, which can result in poor health outcomes.

3. Quality: Another pitfall of healthcare is the quality of care that people receive. Not all healthcare providers or facilities provide the same level of care, and patients may receive suboptimal or inadequate treatment. This can lead to adverse health outcomes and a lack of trust in the healthcare system.

4. Misdiagnosis: In some cases, patients may be misdiagnosed by healthcare providers, leading to unnecessary treatments or delays in receiving the correct diagnosis and treatment. Misdiagnosis can also result in a worsening of the patient's condition and may require additional medical interventions.

5. Side Effects: Finally, some healthcare treatments and medications can have side effects that can be challenging to manage or may cause additional health problems. Patients may need to weigh the benefits and risks of treatment carefully and work closely with their healthcare provider to manage any side effects.

Overall, while healthcare is critical for maintaining good health, it is essential to be aware of the potential pitfalls and work to address them to ensure the best possible outcomes for patients.

Healthcare provides many benefits to individuals and communities. Some of the key benefits of healthcare include:

1. Preventing illnesses: Healthcare enables individuals to receive preventative care such as vaccinations, regular check-ups, and screenings for diseases, which can help prevent illnesses before they occur.

2. Treating illnesses: Healthcare also enables individuals to receive treatment for acute and chronic illnesses, such as infections, injuries, and chronic conditions like diabetes and heart disease. Early detection and treatment of illnesses can improve outcomes and prevent complications.

3. Improving quality of life: Access to healthcare and medical treatments can improve individuals' quality of life by reducing pain, managing symptoms, and improving physical and mental functioning.

4. Increasing life expectancy: Advances in healthcare, such as medical treatments and technologies, have significantly increased life expectancy globally. People are living longer and healthier lives due to access to healthcare.

5. Boosting the economy: Healthcare is a significant contributor to the economy, providing employment opportunities and contributing to economic growth. Access to healthcare can also reduce productivity losses due to illness, keeping people healthy and able to work.

6. Reducing healthcare disparities: Healthcare can help reduce disparities in health outcomes between different populations.

Access to healthcare, preventative care, and treatment can help address inequalities in health outcomes.

Overall, healthcare is a crucial component of a healthy and thriving society. It provides many benefits to individuals and communities, including preventing illnesses, treating illnesses, improving quality of life, increasing life expectancy, boosting the economy, and reducing healthcare disparities.

Saving for healthcare can be an essential aspect of financial planning. Healthcare costs can be significant, and unexpected medical expenses can quickly deplete savings if not adequately planned for. Here are some tips on how to save for healthcare:

1. Create a budget: Start by creating a budget to track your income and expenses. This will help you identify areas where you can cut back on spending to free up money for healthcare savings.

2. Open a healthcare savings account: Consider opening a healthcare savings account (HSA) if you are eligible. An HSA is a tax-advantaged account that allows you to save money for medical expenses, and the funds in the account can be used tax-free for qualifying medical expenses.

3. Contribute to a flexible spending account: If your employer offers a flexible spending account (FSA), consider contributing to it. FSAs are another tax-advantaged account that allows you to save money for medical expenses.

4. Estimate healthcare costs: Estimate your healthcare costs for the year based on your current healthcare needs and potential future expenses. This will help you determine how much you need to save.

5. Consider insurance coverage: Make sure you have adequate insurance coverage to protect you from unexpected medical expenses. Review your insurance policy and make sure you understand your coverage and any out-of-pocket expenses you may be responsible for.

6. Use coupons and discounts: Look for coupons and discounts for medical services and prescriptions to reduce your out-of-pocket expenses.

7. Live a healthy lifestyle: Living a healthy lifestyle can help reduce your healthcare costs by preventing or managing chronic illnesses. Eat a healthy diet, exercise regularly, and practice stress-reduction techniques to promote overall health and wellness.

By following these tips, you can save for healthcare and be better prepared for unexpected medical expenses.

There are many situations where an individual may need healthcare, including:

1. Preventative care: Preventative care is essential for maintaining good health and preventing illnesses. Regular check-ups, vaccinations, and screenings for diseases can help detect health issues early and prevent them from becoming more severe.

2. Acute illnesses: Acute illnesses, such as colds, flu, and infections, can require medical attention. Symptoms such as fever, persistent cough, or severe pain should prompt a visit to a healthcare provider.

3. Chronic conditions: Chronic conditions, such as diabetes, heart disease, and asthma, require ongoing medical management. Regular medical appointments, monitoring, and medication management are critical for managing chronic conditions and preventing complications.

4. Injuries: Injuries, such as broken bones, cuts, and burns, may require medical attention, including X-rays, stitches, and medications to manage pain and prevent infection.

5. Mental health concerns: Mental health concerns, such as depression, anxiety, and substance abuse, require medical attention. Mental health treatment may include therapy, medications, or a combination of both.

6. Women's health: Women may require healthcare for reproductive health concerns, such as menstrual problems, pregnancy, and menopause. Regular gynecological exams and screenings for breast and cervical cancer are also essential for women's health.

7. Children's health: Children may require healthcare for routine check-ups, vaccinations, and management of acute illnesses, such as ear infections or asthma. Children with chronic conditions, such as diabetes or developmental disorders, also require ongoing medical management.

Overall, there are many situations where an individual may need healthcare, from routine preventative care to the management of acute and chronic illnesses. It is essential to seek medical attention when necessary to maintain good health and prevent health problems from becoming more severe.

Healthcare costs in the US can vary widely depending on the type of healthcare services needed, the location, and the healthcare provider. In general, healthcare costs in the US tend to be higher than in other developed countries.

According to a 2020 study by the Commonwealth Fund, the average annual healthcare spending per person in the US was $11,072 in 2018, which is significantly higher than the average spending in other developed countries. In comparison, Canada's per capita healthcare spending was $5,689, while the UK's was $4,192.

The cost of healthcare services can vary greatly depending on the type of service. For example, a routine check-up may cost a few hundred dollars, while hospitalization for a serious illness or injury can cost tens or even hundreds of thousands of dollars. Prescription medications can also be costly, with some specialty drugs costing thousands of dollars per month.

The cost of healthcare in the US is a significant burden for many individuals and families, especially those who are uninsured or underinsured. It is essential to consider healthcare costs when planning for personal finances and to seek out affordable healthcare options.

Part 3: VA Benefits

VA benefits refer to the range of benefits provided by the United States Department of Veterans Affairs (VA) to eligible veterans and their families. These benefits are designed to support veterans in various areas such as healthcare, education, housing, disability compensation, and pension benefits.

Here are some of the key VA benefits available to eligible veterans:

1. Healthcare Benefits: VA healthcare provides comprehensive medical care, including primary care, specialized care, and mental health services. Veterans can access VA healthcare facilities or receive care through community providers.

2. Disability Compensation: Veterans who were injured or became ill while on active duty may be eligible for disability compensation. This benefit provides tax-free monthly payments to veterans with disabilities resulting from military service.

3. Education and Training: VA education benefits include the Post-9/11 GI Bill, which provides funding for tuition, housing, and other education-related expenses. The VA also offers vocational rehabilitation and employment services to help veterans transition into civilian careers.

4. Home Loans: VA home loan benefits provide veterans with the opportunity to buy, build, or improve a home with little or no down payment. The VA also provides support to help veterans avoid foreclosure and keep their homes.

5. Pension Benefits: The VA offers pension benefits to eligible veterans who are 65 years or older, or have a permanent and total disability that is not related to their military service.

These are just some examples of the VA benefits available to veterans and their families. The eligibility criteria for these benefits may vary depending on a veteran's service history, disability status, and other factors.

The process of applying for VA benefits can vary depending on the type of benefit you are seeking. However, the following steps can help you get started:

1. Determine your eligibility: Visit the VA website or call the VA to determine your eligibility for VA benefits. Eligibility requirements can vary depending on the benefit you are seeking, so it's important to verify that you qualify.

2. Gather necessary documents: To apply for VA benefits, you will need to provide documentation such as your military discharge papers (DD-214), medical records, and financial information.

3. Choose your VA benefit: Once you know what VA benefits you may be eligible for, decide which benefit you want to apply for.

4. Complete and submit your application: You can apply for VA benefits online through the VA website or by completing a paper application and mailing it to the VA. Make sure to include all necessary documentation with your application.

5. Follow up on your application: After submitting your application, you can check the status of your application online or by calling the VA. The VA may request additional information or

documentation to process your application, so it's important to respond promptly to any requests.

6. Attend any required appointments or exams: Depending on the benefit you are seeking, you may need to attend appointments or exams to verify your eligibility. Make sure to attend any scheduled appointments and provide any requested information to avoid delays in processing your application.

Overall, applying for VA benefits can be a complex and time-consuming process. It's important to be patient, persistent, and thorough when applying for VA benefits to ensure that you receive the benefits you are entitled to.

VA benefits provide a range of important benefits to eligible veterans and their families. Here are some of the key benefits of VA benefits:

1. Healthcare: VA healthcare provides veterans with access to high-quality medical care at little or no cost. This includes primary care, specialized care, mental health services, and prescription drugs. Veterans can receive care at VA facilities or through community providers, depending on their eligibility.

2. Disability Compensation: VA disability compensation provides tax-free monthly payments to veterans who were injured or became ill as a result of their military service. This benefit can help veterans cover the costs of living with a disability, such as medical expenses, housing, and transportation.

3. Education and Training: VA education benefits can help veterans pursue their educational and career goals. The Post-9/11 GI Bill provides funding for tuition, housing, and other education-related expenses. The VA also offers vocational rehabilitation and

employment services to help veterans transition into civilian careers.

4. Home Loans: VA home loan benefits provide veterans with the opportunity to buy, build, or improve a home with little or no down payment. The VA also provides support to help veterans avoid foreclosure and keep their homes.

5. Pension Benefits: The VA offers pension benefits to eligible veterans who are 65 years or older, or have a permanent and total disability that is not related to their military service. This benefit can provide financial support to veterans who are unable to work due to age or disability.

6. Counseling and Support Services: The VA offers a range of counseling and support services to help veterans and their families cope with the challenges of military service. This includes mental health counseling, bereavement counseling, and support for survivors of military sexual trauma.

Overall, VA benefits can provide veterans and their families with important financial, medical, and educational support. These benefits can help veterans achieve their goals, live more comfortable lives, and cope with the challenges of military service.

While VA benefits can provide significant support to eligible veterans and their families, there are also some potential pitfalls to be aware of. Here are a few examples:

1. Eligibility Requirements: VA benefits have strict eligibility requirements that can be difficult to navigate. Veterans may need to provide extensive documentation to verify their eligibility, and

some benefits have specific criteria related to service-connected disabilities or other factors.

2. Application and Processing Times: Applying for VA benefits can be a time-consuming process, and it may take several months or even years to receive a decision on your application. Delays in processing times can also be frustrating, particularly if you are relying on benefits to cover critical expenses.

3. Limited Coverage: While VA benefits can provide significant support, there may be gaps in coverage or limitations on the benefits provided. For example, VA healthcare may not cover certain medical procedures or treatments, and disability compensation may not fully cover all expenses related to a service-connected disability.

4. Access to Care: While VA healthcare provides veterans with access to medical care, there may be long wait times for appointments or limited availability of specialists or services. Veterans in rural areas or with complex medical conditions may have difficulty accessing the care they need.

5. Dependence on VA Benefits: Relying solely on VA benefits may not provide sufficient financial or medical support for veterans and their families. It's important for veterans to explore other sources of support and to plan for the future to ensure long-term financial stability.

Overall, VA benefits can provide important support to eligible veterans and their families. However, it's important to be aware of potential pitfalls and to plan accordingly to ensure that you receive the support you need.

The amount of money that VA benefits pay out can vary widely depending on the type of benefit and the individual's circumstances. Here are a few examples of typical payment amounts for some of the most common types of VA benefits:

1. Disability Compensation: VA disability compensation payments are tax-free and based on the severity of the veteran's service-connected disability. As of 2021, the monthly payment for a veteran with a 100% disability rating is $3,146.42, while the payment for a veteran with a 10% disability rating is $144.14.

2. Pension Benefits: VA pension benefits provide financial support to eligible veterans who are 65 years or older, or who have a permanent and total disability that is not related to their military service. The maximum annual pension rate for a single veteran as of 2021 is $13,931, while the maximum annual pension rate for a married veteran is $18,253.

3. Education and Training: VA education benefits can provide funding for tuition, housing, and other education-related expenses. The Post-9/11 GI Bill provides up to 36 months of benefits, which vary depending on the veteran's length of service and type of education or training pursued.

4. Home Loans: VA home loan benefits can provide up to 100% financing for a home purchase or refinancing, with loan limits that vary by county. In 2021, the loan limit for most counties is $548,250, but it can be higher in areas with a higher cost of living.

It's important to note that these payment amounts are subject to change and may vary based on individual circumstances. Eligibility requirements and payment amounts for VA benefits can be complex, so veterans are encouraged to speak with a VA representative or a veterans' service organization for more information.

Chapter 5: Loans

A loan is a financial instrument that allows individuals or organizations to borrow money from a lender or financial institution. Loans typically involve the borrower receiving a specific amount of money, which they must repay to the lender over a predetermined period of time.

Loans can be used for a wide variety of purposes, such as financing a home, purchasing a car, paying for college tuition, or funding a business. The terms of the loan agreement usually include details about the interest rate, repayment schedule, and any fees or penalties that may apply.

Interest is the cost of borrowing money, typically expressed as a percentage of the amount borrowed. The interest rate on a loan is determined by several factors, such as the borrower's creditworthiness, the length of the loan, and the current market conditions.

The repayment schedule for a loan typically includes both principal and interest payments. The principal is the amount of money borrowed, while the interest is the cost of borrowing that money. The repayment schedule may be structured as monthly payments or as a lump sum payment at the end of the loan term.

There are several types of loans available, including secured loans, unsecured loans, revolving loans, and installment loans. Each type of loan has its own set of requirements and terms, so it is important to carefully consider the options before choosing a loan product.

There are various types of loans available, each with its own set of features and requirements. Here are some of the most common types of loans:

1. Secured loans: Secured loans require the borrower to provide collateral, such as a car or property, to secure the loan. This provides the lender with some level of security in the event that the borrower defaults on the loan.

2. Unsecured loans: Unsecured loans do not require any collateral and are typically based on the borrower's creditworthiness. These loans can be more difficult to obtain, but may have lower interest rates and more flexible terms.

3. Revolving loans: Revolving loans are lines of credit that can be accessed as needed, up to a predetermined credit limit. These loans are often used for business purposes and can be helpful for managing cash flow.

4. Installment loans: Installment loans involve the borrower receiving a lump sum of money, which is then repaid in regular installments over a set period of time. Mortgages, car loans, and personal loans are all examples of installment loans.

5. Payday loans: Payday loans are short-term loans that are typically used to cover unexpected expenses. These loans often come with high interest rates and fees and should only be used as a last resort.

6. Student loans: Student loans are used to finance higher education and come in two main types: federal student loans and private student loans. Federal student loans typically offer lower interest rates and more flexible repayment options.

7. Business loans: Business loans are used to finance business-related expenses, such as starting a new business, expanding an existing business, or purchasing equipment. These loans can be secured or unsecured and may require a business plan or other documentation.

It is important to carefully consider the type of loan that best fits your needs and to thoroughly understand the terms and conditions of the loan before signing any agreements.

People take out loans for a wide range of reasons, such as to finance large purchases, cover unexpected expenses, or invest in their future. Here are some of the most common reasons why people take out loans:

1. Home purchases: One of the most common reasons people take out loans is to purchase a home. Mortgages are long-term loans that allow individuals to buy a house while making payments over a period of 15 to 30 years.

2. Car purchases: Another common reason people take out loans is to purchase a car. Auto loans are typically installment loans with a fixed interest rate and a repayment term of two to seven years.

3. Education expenses: Many people take out student loans to finance their education. These loans can cover tuition, fees, and living expenses, and are often available with lower interest rates than other types of loans.

4. Home renovations: Homeowners may take out loans to finance renovations or repairs to their homes. Home equity loans and home equity lines of credit (HELOCs) are common types of loans used for home renovations.

5. Debt consolidation: Some people take out loans to consolidate multiple debts into a single, more manageable payment. Debt consolidation loans can simplify the repayment process and potentially lower the overall interest rate.

6. Business expenses: Entrepreneurs and small business owners may take out loans to start or expand their businesses. These loans may be used to purchase equipment, hire employees, or cover other business-related expenses.

7. Emergency expenses: Finally, people may take out loans to cover unexpected expenses, such as medical bills, car repairs, or home repairs. In some cases, these loans may be available with same-day funding or other fast turnaround times.

It's important to note that taking out a loan should always be carefully considered and thoughtfully planned. Before taking out any loan, it's important to understand the interest rates, repayment terms, and any associated fees to make sure the loan is affordable and the right choice for your financial situation.

A low credit score can indicate a higher risk of default to the lender. A low credit score can be the result of late payments, high levels of debt, or a history of bankruptcy or foreclosure. Lenders use credit scores as one of the factors to determine the risk of lending money to a borrower. If a borrower has a low credit score, the lender may view them as a higher risk and may deny the loan application or offer a loan with higher interest rates. However, it's worth noting that different lenders have different credit score requirements and some may be more willing to work with borrowers who have lower credit scores.

To take out a loan, the following documents are typically required:

1. Personal identification: A government-issued photo ID such as a driver's license, passport, or national ID card is usually required to prove your identity.
2. Proof of income: Documents that prove your income, such as recent pay stubs, W-2 forms, or tax returns.
3. Employment verification: A document from your employer that confirms your employment status and salary.
4. Credit history: Your credit report and credit score are used by lenders to determine your creditworthiness, so you may need to provide authorization for the lender to access your credit report.
5. Bank statements: Recent bank statements that show your account balance and transaction history.
6. Collateral documents: If you are taking out a secured loan, such as a car loan or home equity loan, you may need to provide documents that prove ownership of the collateral.
7. Loan application: The lender will require you to fill out a loan application, which will include information about the loan amount, repayment terms, and purpose of the loan.

It's important to note that the specific documents required may vary depending on the type of loan and the lender's requirements. It's always a good idea to check with the lender in advance to confirm their requirements.

Cost of Money

The cost of money is the amount of interest or other fees that a borrower pays to a lender in exchange for the use of borrowed funds. The cost of money can vary depending on a number of factors, including the current economic conditions, the creditworthiness of the borrower, and the type of loan or financial instrument being used.

In general, the cost of money is determined by the interest rate that a lender charges. Interest rates are set by central banks and can vary over time, depending on the state of the economy and other factors. When interest rates are low, borrowing money is typically cheaper, while when interest rates are high, borrowing becomes more expensive.

The cost of money can also be influenced by the creditworthiness of the borrower. Borrowers who have a good credit history and a high credit score are generally considered less risky and may be able to secure loans at lower interest rates. Conversely, borrowers with a poor credit history or low credit score may be charged higher interest rates to compensate for the increased risk of default.

Finally, the type of loan or financial instrument being used can also affect the cost of money. For example, secured loans, which are backed by collateral such as a house or car, typically have lower interest rates than unsecured loans, which do not have any collateral backing. Similarly, credit cards and other types of revolving credit often have higher interest rates than installment loans, which are repaid in fixed payments over a set period of time.

Overall, the cost of money is an important consideration for borrowers, as it can significantly impact the affordability and feasibility of borrowing funds. It is important for borrowers to carefully evaluate the terms and conditions of any loan or financial instrument before agreeing to it, in order to ensure that they fully understand the cost of money and are able to manage their debt effectively.

While borrowing money can provide a necessary source of funding for individuals and businesses, there are also several pitfalls associated with the cost of money. Here are some of the most common pitfalls that borrowers should be aware of:

1. Higher debt burden: The cost of money can lead to higher levels of debt, as borrowers may be tempted to take out more loans than they can comfortably afford to repay. This can result in a debt

burden that is difficult to manage, and can lead to financial stress and hardship.

2. Risk of default: If borrowers are unable to make their loan payments on time, they may risk defaulting on their loans. Defaulting can have serious consequences, such as damage to credit scores, legal action from lenders, and even foreclosure or repossession of assets.

3. Hidden fees: Lenders may charge hidden fees or penalties that are not disclosed upfront, leading to higher overall costs for borrowers. These fees can include origination fees, prepayment penalties, and other charges that can add up over time.

4. Variable interest rates: Some loans have variable interest rates that can change over time, leading to uncertainty and potentially higher costs for borrowers. This can make it difficult to budget for loan payments and can result in unexpected increases in the cost of borrowing.

5. High-interest rates: Borrowers with poor credit scores or limited credit history may be charged higher interest rates, which can make borrowing more expensive and difficult to manage. This can lead to a cycle of debt and financial hardship that can be difficult to escape.

Overall, it is important for borrowers to carefully evaluate the costs and risks associated with borrowing money, and to make informed decisions about their borrowing needs and ability to repay. By understanding the pitfalls of the cost of money, borrowers can make better decisions about their finances and avoid costly mistakes.

Hidden Fees

Hidden fees are charges or costs associated with a loan or financial product that are not clearly disclosed upfront to the borrower. These fees can add up quickly and significantly increase the overall cost of borrowing, making it important for borrowers to carefully read the fine print and understand all the terms and conditions of any loan agreement.

Some common types of hidden fees that borrowers may encounter include:

1. Origination fees: These are fees charged by lenders to cover the costs associated with processing and approving a loan application. Origination fees can be a percentage of the loan amount or a flat fee, and may not be clearly disclosed upfront.

2. Prepayment penalties: Some loans may include penalties for paying off the loan early or making extra payments. These fees can add up over time and make it more difficult for borrowers to pay off their loans ahead of schedule.

3. Late fees: If borrowers fail to make payments on time, lenders may charge late fees or penalties that can significantly increase the overall cost of the loan. These fees may not be clearly disclosed upfront, making it important for borrowers to understand the consequences of missing a payment.

4. Annual fees: Some credit cards and other financial products may include annual fees that are not clearly disclosed upfront. These fees can add up over time and increase the overall cost of using the product.

5. Hidden interest rates: Some loans may have variable interest rates that can change over time, or may include hidden fees or charges that are not clearly disclosed. Borrowers should carefully read the

terms and conditions of any loan agreement to ensure that they fully understand the costs associated with borrowing.

Overall, hidden fees can significantly increase the cost of borrowing and make it more difficult for borrowers to manage their debt. It is important for borrowers to carefully read and understand all the terms and conditions of any loan or financial product, and to ask questions if anything is unclear or confusing. By being aware of hidden fees and charges, borrowers can make informed decisions about their finances and avoid costly surprises down the line.

Part 1: Types of Loans

Secured Loan

A secured loan is a type of loan that requires the borrower to pledge some type of collateral to the lender as security for the loan. The collateral can be any asset that has value, such as a house, car, stocks, or bonds. In the event that the borrower defaults on the loan, the lender has the right to seize the collateral and sell it to recover the amount of the loan.

Secured loans are often used to finance large purchases, such as a car or a house. Because the lender has the security of the collateral, they are generally willing to offer lower interest rates and more favorable terms than they would with an unsecured loan.

Here are some of the most common types of secured loans:

1. Mortgages: Mortgages are secured loans that are used to purchase a home. The home itself serves as collateral for the loan.

2. Auto loans: Auto loans are secured loans that are used to purchase a car. The car itself serves as collateral for the loan.

3. Home equity loans: Home equity loans are secured loans that allow homeowners to borrow against the equity in their homes. The home serves as collateral for the loan.

4. Secured personal loans: Some lenders offer secured personal loans that are backed by collateral, such as a savings account or a car.

Secured loans can be a good option for borrowers who need to borrow a large amount of money and have the ability to pledge collateral. However, it's important to remember that if the borrower defaults on the loan, they risk losing the collateral. As such, it's important to make sure that the borrower is able to make the loan payments on time and in full to avoid defaulting on the loan.

Unsecured Loans

Unsecured loans are loans that do not require the borrower to pledge any collateral or security. Instead, these loans are typically approved based on the borrower's creditworthiness, income, and other financial factors.

Unsecured loans are often used for smaller purchases or expenses, such as home repairs, medical bills, or debt consolidation.

Here are some common types of unsecured loans:

1. Personal loans: Personal loans are unsecured loans that can be used for a variety of purposes, such as debt consolidation, home improvements, or unexpected expenses. These loans typically have higher interest rates than secured loans, but they do not require any collateral.

2. Credit cards: Credit cards are a common type of unsecured loan that allow borrowers to make purchases up to a certain credit limit without needing to provide any collateral. The borrower is required to make minimum monthly payments on the balance, and interest is charged on any unpaid balance.

3. Student loans: Federal student loans are unsecured loans that are used to finance higher education. These loans typically have lower interest rates than other types of loans and offer flexible repayment options.

4. Personal lines of credit: Personal lines of credit are unsecured loans that provide borrowers with access to a set amount of funds that can be used as needed. The borrower only pays interest on the amount borrowed and can draw from the line of credit as needed.

Unsecured loans can be a good option for borrowers who do not have any collateral to offer or do not want to risk losing their assets. However, because these loans do not have collateral to secure them, they typically have higher interest rates than secured loans. Additionally, unsecured loans may have stricter eligibility requirements, such as a higher credit score or income level, to qualify for the loan.

Revolving Loans

Revolving loans are a type of credit account that allows borrowers to make charges, pay them off, and then make charges again. They are also sometimes referred to as open-end credit, because they do not have a fixed repayment term like installment loans. Instead, the borrower can continue to use the line of credit as long as they make payments on time and do not exceed their credit limit.

Here are some common types of revolving loans:

1. Credit cards: Credit cards are the most common type of revolving loan. The borrower is given a credit limit and can make purchases up to that limit. The borrower is required to make minimum payments on the balance each month, and interest is charged on any unpaid balance.

2. Home equity lines of credit (HELOCs): HELOCs are revolving loans that allow homeowners to borrow against the equity in their homes. The borrower can withdraw funds as needed, up to the credit limit, and repay the balance over time.

3. Personal lines of credit: Personal lines of credit are similar to HELOCs, but do not require any collateral. The borrower can withdraw funds as needed and repay the balance over time.

4. Business lines of credit: Business lines of credit are revolving loans that allow business owners to access funds as needed to cover expenses or take advantage of opportunities. The borrower can withdraw funds up to the credit limit and repay the balance over time.

Revolving loans can be a flexible and convenient way to access credit, but they can also be more expensive than other types of loans because of their variable interest rates. Additionally, because there is no fixed repayment term, it can be easy for borrowers to fall into debt if they do not manage their accounts carefully. As with any type of loan, it's important to carefully consider the terms and conditions before taking out a revolving loan, and to make sure that you have a plan in place to repay the balance over time.

Installment Loans

Installment loans are a type of loan that is repaid over a fixed period of time through a series of regular payments, or installments. Each installment includes both principal and interest, so the loan balance decreases over time as the borrower makes payments.

Here are some common types of installment loans:

1. Auto loans: Auto loans are installment loans that are used to finance the purchase of a car. The borrower makes monthly payments until the loan is fully repaid.

2. Mortgages: Mortgages are installment loans that are used to finance the purchase of a home. The borrower makes monthly payments until the loan is fully repaid.

3. Personal loans: Personal loans are installment loans that can be used for a variety of purposes, such as debt consolidation, home improvements, or unexpected expenses. The borrower makes monthly payments until the loan is fully repaid.

4. Student loans: Student loans are installment loans that are used to finance higher education. The borrower makes monthly payments until the loan is fully repaid.

Installment loans can be a good option for borrowers who need to borrow a larger amount of money and want the predictability of fixed monthly payments. Because the loan balance decreases over time, borrowers can see a clear path to paying off the loan. Additionally, installment loans typically have lower interest rates than revolving loans, making them a more affordable option in the long run.

However, it's important to remember that missing payments or defaulting on an installment loan can have serious consequences, such as damage to your credit score and potential legal action from the lender. As with any type of loan, it's important to carefully consider the terms and conditions before taking out an installment loan and to make sure that you have a plan in place to repay the loan over time.

Payday Loans

Payday loans are a type of short-term loan that is typically used to cover unexpected expenses or bridge a gap between paychecks. They are usually for small amounts, typically less than $500, and are due to be repaid in full by the borrower's next payday, usually within two to four weeks.

Payday loans are typically easy to obtain, as they often do not require a credit check and can be applied for online or in-person at payday loan storefronts. However, they come with extremely high interest rates and fees, which can make them very expensive.

The interest rates on payday loans are often expressed in terms of APR (annual percentage rate), which can be several hundred percent. For example, a $100 payday loan with a two-week term might have an APR of 400%. This means that if the borrower cannot repay the loan on time, they can quickly accumulate additional fees and interest, making it even more difficult to repay the loan.

Because of their high interest rates and short repayment terms, payday loans can be very risky for borrowers. In fact, many states have enacted laws to limit the interest rates and fees that payday lenders can charge, or to prohibit payday lending altogether.

If you are considering a payday loan, it's important to carefully consider the risks and to explore other options, such as borrowing from family or friends, using a credit card, or applying for a personal loan from a bank or credit union. If you do decide to take out a payday loan, make sure you understand the terms and conditions and have a plan in place to repay the loan on time.

Student Loans

Student loans are loans that are used to finance higher education, such as college or graduate school. They are typically offered by the government, as well as private lenders, and must be repaid with interest.

There are two main types of student loans: federal student loans and private student loans.

1. Federal student loans: These loans are offered by the U.S. Department of Education and are available to eligible students and their parents. There are several types of federal student loans, including Direct Subsidized Loans, Direct Unsubsidized Loans, and PLUS Loans. The interest rates on federal student loans are typically lower than those on private student loans, and repayment terms are often more flexible.

2. Private student loans: These loans are offered by private lenders, such as banks or credit unions. They may have higher interest rates and fewer repayment options than federal student loans, but may be an option for borrowers who do not qualify for federal student loans or need to borrow more than the federal limits.

When borrowing student loans, it's important to carefully consider the terms and conditions and to borrow only what you need. You should also explore options for scholarships, grants, and work-study programs that can help reduce the amount you need to borrow. It's also important to have a plan in place for repaying your student loans after graduation, as defaulting on a student loan can have serious consequences, such as damage to your credit score and potential legal action from the lender.

Business Loans

Business loans are loans that are used to finance business operations or investments. They are typically offered by banks, credit unions, or other lenders, and can be secured or unsecured, depending on the borrower's creditworthiness and the amount of the loan.

Here are some common types of business loans:

1. Term loans: Term loans are a type of loan that is repaid over a fixed period of time, usually with a set interest rate. They are often used to finance long-term investments, such as buying equipment or expanding a business.

2. Lines of credit: Lines of credit are a type of loan that provides a business with a pool of funds that can be drawn upon as needed. Interest is only charged on the amount borrowed, making them a flexible financing option for businesses with fluctuating cash flow.

3. SBA loans: SBA loans are loans that are guaranteed by the U.S. Small Business Administration. They are often used by small businesses that may not qualify for traditional loans, and typically have lower interest rates and longer repayment terms.

4. Invoice financing: Invoice financing is a type of loan that allows businesses to borrow money against unpaid invoices. This can provide a source of cash flow while waiting for customers to pay their invoices.

When considering a business loan, it's important to carefully consider the terms and conditions, including the interest rate, repayment period, and any fees associated with the loan. It's also important to have a solid business plan in place that outlines how the funds will be used and how the loan will be repaid.

Part 2: Uses of Loans

Car Loans

To get a car loan, you will typically need to provide the lender with information about your income, credit history, and the vehicle you wish to purchase. The lender will use this information to determine your loan amount, interest rate, and other terms. You will also need to provide proof of income and insurance. You can apply for a car loan through a bank, credit union, or online lender. It's also a good idea to shop around and compare rates from different lenders to ensure you get the best deal. Additionally, you should consider your budget and only borrow what you can afford to repay.

There are several reasons why someone may be denied a car loan, some of the main reasons are:

1. Poor credit score: A low credit score can indicate a higher risk of default to the lender, which can result in a denied loan application.
2. Insufficient income: Lenders typically require borrowers to have a steady income to repay the loan. If you don't have a stable income, or your income is not high enough, the lender may deny your loan application.
3. High debt-to-income ratio: Lenders will look at how much debt you already have compared to your income. If you have too much debt, it may be difficult for you to take on another loan.
4. Lack of credit history: If you have no credit history, lenders may be unable to determine your creditworthiness and may deny your loan application.
5. Lack of proof of income or employment: Lenders will want to verify your income and employment status to ensure that you can afford the loan payments.
6. The car you want to buy is older or has high mileage, or is considered a high-risk vehicle, the lender may not want to finance it.
7. Recent bankruptcies or foreclosures, or other financial issues, can also make it difficult for you to get approved for a car loan.

It is worth noting that different lenders have different criteria for loan approval, so if you are denied a loan from one lender, it may be worth trying another lender.

There is no one definitive answer to what the easiest way to get a car loan is, as it can vary depending on an individual's financial situation and credit history. However, here are a few suggestions that may increase your chances of getting approved for a car loan:

1. Improve your credit score: Your credit score is one of the most important factors that lenders consider when evaluating a car loan application. By taking steps to improve your credit score, such as paying your bills on time and reducing your outstanding debt, you may increase your chances of getting approved for a loan.
2. Shop around: Different lenders have different credit score requirements and interest rates. By shopping around, you can compare rates and terms and find a lender that is willing to work with your credit situation.
3. Consider a co-signer: If you have a poor credit score, a co-signer with good credit may increase your chances of getting approved for a car loan.
4. Down payment: Making a down payment can lower the loan amount and the risk for the lender, which may increase your chances of getting approved for a car loan.
5. Get pre-approved: Before you start shopping for a car, consider getting pre-approved for a loan. This will give you a better idea of how much you can afford to spend and may increase your chances of getting approved for a loan.

It's also worth noting that some lenders specialize in working with borrowers who have poor credit, so you may want to consider working with one of these lenders.

A co-signer with good credit can increase your chances of getting approved for a car loan if you have poor credit. A co-signer is someone who agrees to take on the responsibility of repaying the loan if you are unable to do so. By having a co-signer with good credit, it can help to mitigate the risk for the lender and increase your chances of getting approved for the loan. Keep in mind that the co-signer will also be responsible for the loan and any missed payments will affect their credit as well. It's important to communicate with your co-signer, to make sure they understand the responsibility they are taking on, and that you have a plan to repay the loan on time.

Making a down payment can help to lower the loan amount and the risk for the lender, which can increase your chances of getting approved for a car loan. A down payment is a lump sum of money that you pay up front when you purchase a vehicle. By making a down payment, you can reduce the amount you need to borrow, which can help to lower the risk for the lender.

It also shows the lender that you are financially responsible and have the means to make a significant investment in the car, which may make them more willing to approve your loan. Additionally, making a down payment can also help to lower your monthly car payments and overall interest costs. The amount of down payment required varies from lender to lender, it's a good idea to check with the lender and see what their specific requirements are. However, it's worth noting that in some cases, a down payment is not required and the loan can be 100% financed.

Getting pre-approved for a loan can be beneficial before you start shopping for a car. Pre-approval means that a lender has reviewed your credit and financial information, and has given you a preliminary approval for a loan up to a certain amount.

Getting pre-approved can give you a better idea of how much you can afford to spend on a car, and can also help you negotiate a better price with the dealership. Additionally, it also shows the dealer that you are a serious buyer and that you have the means to purchase the car which they may consider while finalizing the deal.

Moreover, It also allows you to compare rates and terms from different lenders and find the best deal for you before making a final decision. Keep in mind that pre-approval is not the same as final approval, the lender will still need to review the specific car you want to purchase and the final loan amount may change. However, pre-approval can give you a better idea of what to expect and increase your chances of getting approved for a car loan.

Personal Loans

A personal loan is a type of unsecured loan that provides an individual with funds for personal use, such as paying off debt, financing a home improvement project, or covering unexpected expenses. The loan is not secured by any property or collateral and is typically offered by banks, credit unions, and online lenders. The amount borrowed, repayment period, and interest rate are typically determined based on the borrower's credit score and income. Repayment of the loan is usually made through fixed monthly payments, with the principal and interest paid back over a specified period of time.

A personal loan can be taken out for various reasons, including:

1. Debt consolidation: To pay off high-interest credit card debt or multiple bills with a single loan at a lower interest rate.

2. Home improvements: To finance renovations or upgrades to a property.

3. Unexpected expenses: To cover emergency costs such as medical bills, car repairs, or travel expenses.

4. Wedding expenses: To pay for wedding-related costs such as a venue, catering, or a honeymoon.

5. Education: To finance education-related expenses such as tuition or books.

6. Business expenses: To cover business costs such as purchasing inventory, equipment, or advertising.

7. Vacation: To finance a trip or vacation.

8. Consolidating student loans: To refinance and pay off student loan debt at a lower interest rate.

9. Moving expenses: To cover the costs of relocating, such as hiring movers or renting a truck.

10. Auto loans: To finance the purchase of a vehicle.

It's important to consider the cost of the loan, including the interest rate and fees, and the ability to repay the loan before taking out a personal loan.

Here are some of the potential pitfalls of taking out a personal loan:

1. High interest rates: Personal loans can have higher interest rates than secured loans, such as a mortgage or auto loan, and can make it more expensive to borrow money.

2. Fees: Some personal loans may come with origination fees, prepayment penalties, or other fees that can add to the overall cost of borrowing.

3. Repayment terms: Personal loans typically have a set repayment period, and missing payments or paying late can result in additional fees or a higher interest rate.

4. Credit score impact: Taking out a personal loan can impact a person's credit score, especially if they have a limited credit history or make late payments.

5. Debt trap: Taking out a personal loan to consolidate debt or cover unexpected expenses can lead to taking on additional debt if the root cause of the financial problem is not addressed.

6. Limited use of funds: Personal loans are typically used for specific purposes and may not be ideal for larger investments or long-term financial planning.

7. Lack of collateral: Unlike secured loans, personal loans are not backed by collateral and therefore carry a higher risk for the

lender. This risk can result in higher interest rates or stricter loan terms for the borrower.

Before taking out a personal loan, it's important to carefully consider the terms and conditions of the loan, as well as the borrower's ability to repay the loan in a timely manner.

Student Loans

To get a student loan, one needs to follow these steps:

1. Research and compare different loan options from government and private sources.
2. Complete the Free Application for Federal Student Aid (FAFSA) to determine eligibility for federal loans.
3. If approved, accept the loan offer and complete any additional requirements, such as loan counseling or entrance counseling.
4. If necessary, apply for private loans from banks or other financial institutions.
5. Review and sign the loan agreement, indicating the terms and conditions of the loan.
6. Use the loan funds to pay for education expenses such as tuition, books, and housing.

It's important to understand the terms and conditions of the loan, as well as your responsibilities for repaying the loan after graduation.

The Free Application for Federal Student Aid (FAFSA) is a form used to apply for financial aid from the federal government to help pay for college. It is a comprehensive application that collects information about a student's and their family's financial situation to determine their eligibility for federal student aid programs, such as grants, scholarships, and loans.

To complete the FAFSA, you will need to provide information about your income, assets, and other financial resources. You may also need to provide information about your family's financial situation, including the income and assets of your parents or other financial supporters.

Once you have submitted the FAFSA, the government will process the application and determine your eligibility for financial aid. This can include grants, work-study programs, and loans. The results of the FAFSA will be used by colleges to determine your eligibility for aid from their own programs as well.

It's important to note that the FAFSA must be completed annually to maintain eligibility for federal financial aid, and the application period for the FAFSA usually opens on October 1st and closes on the federal deadline, usually in the spring.

Loan counseling and entrance counseling are mandatory sessions for students who have been approved for federal student loans. These sessions are designed to educate students about their rights and responsibilities as borrowers, and to help them understand the terms and conditions of their loans.

Entrance counseling is a one-time requirement that must be completed before a student can receive their first disbursement of federal student loans. During entrance counseling, students learn about the loan process, including interest rates, loan repayment options, and the consequences of default. They will also be given an opportunity to ask questions and clarify any concerns about their loan.

Loan counseling, on the other hand, is required annually for students who are receiving federal student loans. During loan counseling, students will receive updates on their loan balances, interest rates, and other loan-related information. They will also be reminded of their rights and responsibilities as borrowers and be given the opportunity to ask questions about their loans.

Both entrance counseling and loan counseling can be completed online, and are important steps in ensuring that students understand their loan obligations and are prepared to manage their debt effectively.

To get a non-federal student loan, you can follow these steps:

1. Research different private loan options: Compare interest rates, repayment terms, and other loan features from different lenders to find the best option for you.

2. Check your credit score: Your credit score and credit history will impact your loan options and interest rates. You can check your credit score for free from several websites.

3. Apply for a loan: You can apply for a private student loan directly through a lender or through a loan marketplace. You will need to provide personal and financial information, including information about your income and assets.

4. Review and accept the loan offer: If approved, you will receive a loan offer from the lender, detailing the interest rate, repayment terms, and other loan features. Review the offer carefully and make sure you understand the terms and conditions of the loan before accepting.

5. Complete the loan disbursement process: Once you have accepted the loan offer, the lender will disburse the loan funds to your school. The funds will be used to pay for tuition, books, and other education-related expenses.

It's important to consider the terms and conditions of private loans carefully, as they may have higher interest rates and stricter repayment terms compared to federal loans. It's also recommended to exhaust all other financial aid options before taking out a private student loan.

Getting a federal student loan involves a series of steps that are relatively straightforward. Here's a general overview of the process:

1. Complete the Free Application for Federal Student Aid (FAFSA): The first step in applying for a federal student loan is to fill out the FAFSA. This application will determine your eligibility for various types of financial aid, including federal student loans.

2. Review your financial aid package: After you submit the FAFSA, your school will send you a financial aid package that outlines the types and amounts of aid you're eligible to receive. This package may include federal student loans, grants, scholarships, and work-study opportunities.

3. Accept or decline your federal student loans: If you're offered a federal student loan as part of your financial aid package, you'll need to review the terms and conditions of the loan and decide whether or not to accept it. Make sure to carefully consider the interest rate, repayment terms, and any associated fees before accepting the loan.

4. Complete loan entrance counseling: If you're a first-time borrower of a federal student loan, you'll need to complete loan entrance counseling before you can receive your loan funds. This counseling will help you understand the terms of your loan and your responsibilities as a borrower.

5. Sign a Master Promissory Note (MPN): To receive a federal student loan, you'll need to sign an MPN, which is a legal document that outlines the terms and conditions of your loan. You'll only need to sign this document once, and it will be used for all of your federal student loans while you're in school.

6. Receive your loan funds: Once you've completed all of the above steps, your federal student loan funds will be disbursed directly to your school to pay for your tuition, fees, and other educational expenses. If there are any funds left over after your school has been paid, they will be refunded to you.

Overall, the process of getting a federal student loan is relatively straightforward, but it's important to carefully consider the terms and conditions of the loan before accepting it. Make sure to review all of your financial aid options and choose the option that best fits your needs and budget.

Mortgages

A mortgage is a type of loan that is typically used to purchase real estate, such as a home, apartment, or commercial property. When you take out a mortgage, the lender (usually a bank or financial institution) will provide you with a lump sum of money, which you will use to buy the property.

The mortgage is secured by the property itself, which means that if you are unable to make your payments, the lender has the right to take possession of the property and sell it to recoup their losses. This makes mortgages a relatively low-risk type of loan for lenders, which is why they are typically offered at lower interest rates than other types of loans.

Mortgages come in a variety of types and structures. The most common types of mortgages are fixed-rate mortgages, in which the interest rate stays the same for the entire term of the loan, and adjustable-rate mortgages, in which the interest rate can fluctuate over time.

The term of a mortgage can also vary, but most mortgages have a term of 15 to 30 years. During this time, you will make monthly payments to the lender, which will include both principal (the amount you borrowed) and interest (the fee charged by the lender for lending you the money).

Overall, a mortgage is a major financial commitment and requires careful consideration and planning before taking on the responsibility of a long-term loan.

A mortgage is a loan used to purchase a property and there are several benefits to obtaining a mortgage, including:

1. Ability to purchase a property: A mortgage allows individuals to purchase a property that they may not be able to afford with cash.
2. Building equity: As the mortgage is paid off, the homeowner builds equity in the property. This equity can be used as a source of income during retirement or as a down payment on a future home.
3. Potential appreciation of the property: Real estate values can appreciate over time, which can increase the value of the property and the homeowner's equity.
4. Tax benefits: Mortgage interest is tax-deductible, which can lower the overall cost of homeownership. Property taxes are also tax-deductible in most cases.

5. Forced savings: A mortgage can act as a forced savings plan, as the homeowner is required to make regular payments towards the mortgage, which helps them to save money.
6. Sense of community: Being a homeowner generally gives a sense of community and belonging, people may feel more connected to the neighborhood and tend to take better care of the property.

It's important to note that a mortgage also has risks, such as the possibility of foreclosing if payments are not made, and the interest rate can change over time.

Equity refers to the value of a property that the owner has an interest in. It is calculated as the difference between the property's value and any outstanding loans or mortgages on the property.

For example, if a property is worth $500,000 and the owner has a mortgage of $400,000, the owner's equity in the property is $100,000. If the owner makes payments on the mortgage, the equity will increase as the mortgage balance decreases.

Homeowners can use their equity in several ways, for example:

1. As a down payment on a future home: Homeowners can sell their current property and use the equity as a down payment on a new home.
2. As a source of income: Homeowners can take out a loan against their equity, called a home equity loan or a line of credit. This can be used for home improvements, debt consolidation, or other expenses.
3. As an investment: The equity in a property can also appreciate over time, which can provide a good return on investment for the homeowner.

It's important to note that equity can also decrease if the value of the property falls or if the homeowner takes on additional debt against the property.

There are also several drawbacks or pitfalls of obtaining a mortgage, including:

1. High up-front costs: Obtaining a mortgage requires a significant up-front investment, including a down payment, closing costs, and other fees.
2. Long-term commitment: A mortgage is a long-term commitment, usually lasting 15-30 years, and the homeowner is required to make regular payments during that time.
3. Risk of foreclosure: If the homeowner is unable to make their mortgage payments, they risk losing their property through foreclosure.
4. Interest rate risk: The interest rate on a mortgage can change, which can increase the overall cost of the loan.
5. Limits on flexibility: A mortgage can limit an individual's flexibility to move or make changes to their property, as they are required to continue making payments on the mortgage.
6. Responsibility for maintenance and repairs: As a homeowner, you are responsible for maintaining and repairing the property, which can be costly.
7. Limited liquid assets: If a large portion of your assets are tied to your property, it may limit your ability to access cash in case of an emergency.
8. Limited mobility: Selling a property with a mortgage can be more complicated, and it may limit your ability to move to a new location if you need to.

Part 3: Interest

In finance, interest is the cost of borrowing money or the return on invested capital. Interest can be calculated as a percentage of the principal amount borrowed or invested, and is usually expressed as an annual percentage rate (APR).

When you borrow money, you typically have to pay interest to the lender as compensation for the use of their funds. The interest rate on a loan depends on several factors, including the borrower's creditworthiness, the amount borrowed, the length of the loan term, and current market conditions. The interest rate can be fixed, meaning it stays the same for the entire loan term, or variable, meaning it changes over time based on market conditions.

Interest rates are an important aspect of finance because they affect the cost of borrowing and the return on investment. They can also impact the overall health of the economy. For example, low interest rates can stimulate economic growth by encouraging borrowing and spending, while high interest rates can slow down economic growth by making borrowing more expensive.

Interest rates are the cost of borrowing or the return on lending money. They are typically expressed as a percentage of the principal amount and are charged or earned over a specific period of time, usually on an annual basis. Interest rates are an important tool used by central banks to influence the economy by affecting the cost of borrowing, spending, and investment.

Interest rates can be classified into several categories based on the type of interest rate, the length of the loan term, and the method of calculation. Some common types of interest rates include:

1. Fixed interest rates: These are interest rates that remain the same over the entire length of the loan or investment term. Fixed

interest rates are commonly used in mortgages, personal loans, and bonds.

2. Variable interest rates: These are interest rates that fluctuate over time based on market conditions. Variable interest rates are commonly used in adjustable-rate mortgages, credit cards, and some types of savings accounts.

3. Prime interest rates: These are the interest rates that commercial banks charge their most creditworthy customers. The prime rate is usually used as a benchmark for other types of loans and interest rates.

4. Federal funds rate: This is the interest rate at which commercial banks lend to each other overnight to meet their reserve requirements. The Federal Reserve Bank uses the federal funds rate as a tool to influence the economy by adjusting the money supply and controlling inflation.

5. Annual percentage rate (APR): This is the total cost of borrowing, including both the interest rate and any fees associated with the loan. The APR is used to compare the cost of different types of loans and credit cards.

Interest rates can have a significant impact on the economy, affecting consumer spending, business investment, and inflation. When interest rates are low, borrowing becomes cheaper, which can stimulate spending and investment. However, low interest rates can also lead to inflation and asset bubbles. Conversely, high interest rates can slow down economic growth and borrowing, but can also help control inflation. The balance of interest rates is an important factor in macroeconomic policy and financial decision-making.

The typical APR (Annual Percentage Rate) for earning interest and regular interest rates can vary depending on the type of account, investment, or loan you are considering, as well as market conditions, economic factors, and the issuer's creditworthiness.

For regular interest rates, the APR can also vary depending on the type of loan or credit product you are considering. For example, credit cards often have higher interest rates than personal loans or mortgages, with APRs ranging from 15% to 25% or more. Auto loans and personal loans typically have lower interest rates than credit cards, with APRs ranging from 3% to 10% or more, depending on the borrower's creditworthiness and other factors. Mortgages often have the lowest interest rates of any type of loan, with APRs ranging from 2% to 5% or more, depending on the type of mortgage, the length of the loan term, and market conditions.

It's important to note that interest rates can change over time based on a variety of factors, so it's always a good idea to compare rates from multiple issuers and shop around for the best deal. Additionally, the APR is just one factor to consider when evaluating a financial product - other factors like fees, penalties, and repayment terms should also be taken into account.

Interest rates can be encountered in many different areas of personal finance and investing. Some common places where someone might encounter interest rates include:

1. Savings accounts: When you deposit money into a savings account, the bank or financial institution may pay you interest on your balance.

2. Certificates of deposit (CDs): CDs are a type of investment that allows you to earn interest on your deposit over a fixed period of time.

3. Bonds: Bonds are a type of fixed-income investment that pays interest to investors over the life of the bond.

4. Mortgages: When you take out a mortgage to buy a home, you will be charged interest on the amount you borrow.

5. Auto loans: If you finance a car purchase, you will be charged interest on the loan amount.

6. Credit cards: Credit cards charge interest on balances that are not paid in full by the due date.

7. Personal loans: If you take out a personal loan, you will be charged interest on the loan amount.

8. Student loans: Student loans charge interest on the amount borrowed to finance education expenses.

In addition to these specific financial products, interest rates can also be encountered in the broader economy, such as the interest rates set by central banks, which can influence the cost of borrowing and spending for businesses and individuals alike.

While interest rates can be a useful tool for managing personal finances and investing, there are also several pitfalls and risks associated with them that individuals should be aware of. Some of these pitfalls include:

1. High-interest rates can lead to debt: When interest rates are high, borrowing money becomes more expensive, and individuals may be more likely to take on debt that they are unable to repay.

2. Variable interest rates can be unpredictable: When interest rates are variable, they can be difficult to predict, which can make it challenging for borrowers and investors to plan for the future.

3. Low-interest rates can hurt savings: When interest rates are low, the returns on savings accounts, CDs, and other types of investments may not keep up with inflation, which can erode the value of savings over time.

4. Interest rates can be influenced by external factors: Interest rates can be affected by a variety of external factors, including changes in the economy, monetary policy decisions by central banks, and geopolitical events, which can be difficult to predict.

5. Interest rates can be subject to fees and penalties: In addition to the interest charged on loans and other types of credit, borrowers may also be subject to fees and penalties for late payments, missed payments, or other types of default, which can increase the cost of borrowing.

6. Interest rates can be used to manipulate financial markets: In some cases, interest rates may be used to manipulate financial markets, which can create a volatile and unpredictable environment for investors and borrowers alike.

In general, it is important for individuals to carefully consider the risks and benefits of interest rates before making any financial decisions. By understanding how interest rates work and the potential pitfalls associated with them, individuals can make more informed decisions about their personal finances and investments.

Chapter 6: Investing

Investing is the act of allocating resources, typically money, with the expectation of generating income or profit in the future. The goal of investing is to grow your wealth over time by putting your money into various assets that have the potential to appreciate in value or generate income.

There are many different types of investments available, including stocks, bonds, real estate, mutual funds, and exchange-traded funds (ETFs), among others. Each of these investment options has its own unique characteristics, risks, and potential rewards.

When you invest in something, you are essentially buying a stake in that asset or company. For example, if you invest in stocks, you are buying a small piece of ownership in the company whose stock you have purchased. If the company does well and its stock price increases, the value of your investment will also increase.

Investing requires some level of risk-taking as there is no guarantee that any particular investment will perform as expected or generate the desired return. Therefore, it is important to do your research and understand the risks involved before making any investment decisions. It's also important to have a long-term investment horizon and to diversify your investments to minimize risk.

Ultimately, investing is a way to build wealth over time and achieve your financial goals. Whether you are investing for retirement, to pay for a child's education, or to build a nest egg for the future, the key is to have a well-thought-out investment strategy and to stick with it over the long term.

Investing can provide a variety of benefits, including the potential for long-term growth of wealth, diversification of assets, and the ability to earn passive income. Investing in a diversified portfolio of stocks, bonds, and other assets can also help to spread risk and increase the chances of achieving financial goals. Additionally, investing can also help to beat inflation, which can erode the purchasing power of cash over time. It's important to remember that all investing carries risk and past performance is not indicative of future results. It's always a good idea to consult with a financial advisor before making any investment decisions.

Investing can also have drawbacks, some of which include:

1. Risk: Investing always carries some level of risk, and the potential for loss is always present. There is no guarantee that an investment will perform as expected, and even a well-researched investment can result in a loss.
2. Volatility: The value of investments can fluctuate rapidly, which can make it difficult for investors to know when to buy or sell. This volatility can also cause emotional stress for some investors.
3. Lack of liquidity: Some investments, such as real estate or private company shares, can be difficult to sell quickly, which can limit an investor's flexibility.
4. Hidden fees and charges: Some investments come with hidden fees and charges that can eat into returns, making it difficult to achieve financial goals.
5. Lack of control: Investing means entrusting your money to other people, such as fund managers or company executives. This can make it difficult to have control over the performance of your investments.

It's important to remember that the potential rewards of investing must be balanced against the potential risks and drawbacks. It's always a good idea to consult with a financial advisor before making any investment decisions.

There are many different types of investments available, each with their own unique characteristics and risks. Some of the most common types of investments include:

1. Stocks: These are shares of ownership in a company that are traded on stock exchanges. When you buy a stock, you become a part-owner of the company and are entitled to a share of the company's profits.
2. Bonds: These are debt securities issued by companies or governments. When you buy a bond, you are essentially lending money to the issuer in exchange for interest payments and the return of the principal at maturity.

3. Mutual Funds: These are professionally managed investment portfolios that pool money from many investors to buy a diversified mix of stocks, bonds, and other securities.
4. Exchange-Traded Funds (ETFs): Similar to mutual funds, ETFs are professionally managed investment portfolios that pool money from many investors. ETFs trade on stock exchanges, like individual stocks, and can offer more flexibility and lower costs than traditional mutual funds.
5. Real estate: This includes investments in physical property, such as rental properties, commercial buildings, or raw land.
6. Commodities: These are physical goods, such as precious metals, oil, agricultural products, and other natural resources.
7. Cryptocurrency: Cryptocurrency is a digital or virtual currency that uses cryptography for security. Bitcoin and Ethereum are the most famous examples.
8. Certificates of deposit (CDs): These are time deposits offered by banks and other financial institutions. CDs typically offer higher interest rates than savings accounts but they have limited flexibility

It's important to remember that different types of investments carry different levels of risk, and it's important to understand the characteristics of each type of investment before investing. It's always a good idea to consult with a financial advisor before making any investment decisions.

Part 1: Types of Investment

Stocks

Stocks, also known as equities, are shares of ownership in a company that are traded on stock exchanges. When you buy a stock, you become a part-owner of the company and are entitled to a share of the company's profits. The value of a stock is determined by the market and can fluctuate depending on various factors such as the company's financial performance, market conditions, and overall economic conditions.

There are two main types of stocks: common stocks and preferred stocks. Common stocks represent ownership in a company and entitle the holder to voting rights on important company matters, such as the election of the board of directors. Preferred stocks do not have voting rights, but they typically have a higher priority in the event that the company goes bankrupt and is liquidated.

Stocks can be bought and sold on stock exchanges, such as the New York Stock Exchange (NYSE) and the Nasdaq, through a stockbroker. Stocks can also be bought and sold through online trading platforms.

Investing in stocks can be a good way to earn a return on your investment over the long term, but it also carries some risk. The value of a stock can fluctuate rapidly, and the value of a stock can drop significantly if the company doesn't perform well financially. Additionally, the stock market as a whole can also experience significant volatility and can drop suddenly, as seen during market crashes or recessions.

It's important to remember that when investing in stocks, it's important to have a well-diversified portfolio and not to put all your eggs in one basket. It's also important to have a long-term investment horizon, as stocks tend to perform better over the long-term. It's always a good idea to consult with a financial advisor before making any investment decisions.

Bonds

Bonds are debt securities issued by companies or governments. When you buy a bond, you are essentially lending money to the issuer in exchange for interest payments and the return of the principal at maturity. The issuer of the bond promises to pay you a fixed or variable interest rate over a certain period of time and at the end of the bond term, the issuer will pay back the original amount that was borrowed (face value or principal).

Bonds are considered less risky than stocks, but the risk level can vary depending on the issuer and the type of bond. Bonds issued by the government or large, well-established companies are considered safer than bonds issued by smaller or less financially stable companies.

There are several types of bonds available, including:

1. Treasury Bonds: These are issued by the federal government and are considered to be among the safest investments because they are backed by the full faith and credit of the U.S. government.
2. Corporate Bonds: These are issued by companies and can be further categorized as investment-grade or high-yield bonds. Investment-grade bonds are considered safer than high-yield bonds, which are issued by companies with a higher risk of default.
3. Municipal Bonds: These are issued by state and local governments and are often tax-exempt, which can make them attractive to investors in higher tax brackets.
4. Foreign Bonds: These are bonds issued by foreign governments or companies and can be subject to currency fluctuations and political risks.
5. Floating Rate Bonds: These bonds pay an interest rate that varies with market conditions, instead of fixed interest rate.

The value of a bond can change depending on interest rate movements and the creditworthiness of the issuer. When interest rates rise, bond prices fall, and when interest rates fall, bond prices rise.

It's important to remember that all bonds carry some level of risk and it's important to research the bond issuer and the bond itself before investing.

It's always a good idea to consult with a financial advisor before making any investment decisions.

Mutual Funds

Mutual funds are a type of investment vehicle that pools money from multiple investors to invest in a variety of securities such as stocks, bonds, and other financial assets. These funds are managed by professional portfolio managers who aim to achieve a specific investment objective, such as long-term growth, income generation, or capital preservation.

When you invest in a mutual fund, you are essentially buying a share in the fund, which represents a proportional ownership in the underlying assets held by the fund. The price of the mutual fund share is determined by the total value of the fund's assets divided by the number of shares outstanding.

There are several benefits of investing in mutual funds. Firstly, mutual funds offer diversification, which means that by investing in a mutual fund, you are spreading your investment across a variety of assets, which can help to reduce the risk of losses from any single investment. Additionally, mutual funds provide access to professional money management and research, which can be valuable for investors who lack the time or expertise to manage their own investments.

Mutual funds are available in a variety of types and categories, such as equity funds, bond funds, balanced funds, and sector-specific funds. Each type of mutual fund has its own investment objective, strategy, and risk profile. For example, equity funds invest primarily in stocks and are suited for investors seeking long-term growth, while bond funds invest mainly in fixed-income securities and are suitable for investors seeking regular income with relatively lower risk.

Investors in mutual funds typically pay fees and expenses, including management fees, sales charges, and other administrative costs. These costs can vary depending on the type of fund and the investment management company, and it's important to read the fund's prospectus to understand the fees and expenses associated with the investment.

Overall, mutual funds can be a good option for investors seeking diversification, professional management, and access to a variety of asset classes. However, investors should carefully consider their investment objectives, risk tolerance, and the costs associated with the investment before investing in a mutual fund.

Exchange-Traded Funds

Exchange-traded funds (ETFs) are a type of investment vehicle that combines the features of mutual funds and individual stocks. Like mutual funds, ETFs pool money from multiple investors to invest in a basket of securities such as stocks, bonds, and other financial assets. However, unlike mutual funds, ETFs are traded on an exchange like individual stocks, and their price fluctuates throughout the trading day.

ETFs are designed to track a specific index, such as the S&P 500, or a sector or industry. For example, an ETF that tracks the S&P 500 will hold a basket of stocks that mirrors the performance of the index. When you buy shares in an ETF, you are essentially buying a proportional ownership in the underlying assets held by the fund.

One of the key advantages of ETFs is their flexibility. Because they are traded on an exchange, you can buy and sell ETFs throughout the trading day, just like individual stocks. This means that you can use ETFs to trade short-term market trends, as well as for long-term investment strategies.

ETFs also offer lower expenses than traditional mutual funds. This is because ETFs are passively managed, meaning they track an index, and do not require the same level of active management as mutual funds. As a result, ETFs typically have lower management fees and operating expenses than mutual funds.

Another advantage of ETFs is their tax efficiency. Because they are structured differently than mutual funds, ETFs are generally more tax-efficient, which can be beneficial for investors looking to minimize their tax liability.

Like mutual funds, ETFs come in a variety of types and categories, including equity ETFs, bond ETFs, and sector-specific ETFs. Each type of ETF has its own investment objective, strategy, and risk profile.

Overall, ETFs can be a good option for investors looking for flexible, low-cost investment vehicles that offer broad diversification across different asset classes. However, as with any investment, it's important to carefully consider your investment objectives, risk tolerance, and the costs associated with the investment before investing in an ETF.

Real Estate Investing

Real estate investing involves the acquisition and ownership of physical property, such as rental properties, commercial buildings, or raw land. Real estate can provide a steady stream of income through rent and can also appreciate in value over time.

There are many different types of real estate investments, including:

1. Residential properties: This can include single-family homes, duplexes, triplexes, and multi-unit apartment buildings. Residential properties can be rented out to tenants for a steady stream of income.
2. Commercial properties: This can include office buildings, retail centers, warehouses, and other types of commercial real estate. Commercial properties are typically leased to businesses and can generate income through rent.
3. Raw land: This includes undeveloped land that can be used for a variety of purposes, such as residential or commercial development, farming, or resource extraction.
4. REITs: Real estate Investment Trusts (REITs) are publicly traded companies that own, operate, or finance real estate properties. They allow investors to invest in a diversified portfolio of real estate properties without the need to buy and manage the property themselves.
5. Crowdfunding real estate: This is a newer form of real estate investing that allows investors to pool their money to buy and manage properties.

Real estate investing can be a good way to earn a return on your investment over the long term, but it also carries some risk. The value of real estate can fluctuate based on local market conditions, and the cost of owning and maintaining a property can be significant. Additionally, real estate investments can be highly illiquid and can take time to sell.

It's important to remember that real estate investing requires a significant amount of research, due diligence, and a long-term investment horizon. It's also important to have a well-diversified portfolio and not to put all your eggs in one basket. It's always a good idea to consult with a financial advisor or real estate professional before making any investment decisions.

Commodity Investing

Investing in commodities involves buying and selling raw materials or primary products such as precious metals, energy, agricultural products, and industrial metals. Commodities are a physical asset that can be bought and sold in various markets, including futures, options, and exchange-traded funds (ETFs).

There are several reasons why investors choose to invest in commodities. Firstly, commodities can be a hedge against inflation. As the prices of goods and services rise, the prices of commodities tend to rise as well, which can help to offset the impact of inflation on an investment portfolio. Secondly, commodities can offer diversification, as they tend to have low correlation with stocks and bonds, meaning that they can help to reduce overall portfolio risk.

When investing in commodities, there are several different ways to gain exposure to these assets. One way is to invest directly in the physical commodity itself. For example, investors can buy and store physical gold or silver as a store of value. However, this can be costly and requires specialized knowledge and storage facilities.

Another way to invest in commodities is through futures contracts. A futures contract is an agreement to buy or sell a specific commodity at a specified price and date in the future. Futures contracts are traded on exchanges, and investors can buy and sell these contracts to gain exposure to the underlying commodity. However, futures trading can be complex and involves significant risks, including leverage, which can magnify both gains and losses.

Exchange-traded funds (ETFs) and exchange-traded notes (ETNs) are another way to invest in commodities. These investment vehicles track the price of a particular commodity or group of commodities and can be bought and sold like stocks on an exchange. ETFs and ETNs can offer convenient and cost-effective exposure to commodities, but investors should be aware of the fees and expenses associated with these investments.

Finally, investors can also invest in commodity-related equities, such as mining companies or energy producers. These companies are involved in the production or extraction of commodities, and their performance is typically tied to the price of the underlying commodity. However, these investments also carry risks associated with individual stocks, such as company-specific risks and market volatility.

Overall, investing in commodities can offer diversification and inflation protection to an investment portfolio. However, it is important for investors to carefully consider their investment objectives, risk tolerance, and the costs associated with each investment option before investing in commodities. Additionally, investors should be aware of the unique risks and complexities associated with investing in commodities and should seek professional advice if needed.

Futures

Futures are a type of financial contract that obligates the buyer to purchase an underlying asset, such as a commodity or financial instrument, at a predetermined price and date in the future. Futures contracts are traded on exchanges and are used by investors to speculate on the future price of the underlying asset, as well as to hedge against price volatility.

Futures contracts are standardized agreements that specify the quality, quantity, and delivery date of the underlying asset. For example, a futures contract for crude oil might specify that the buyer will purchase 1,000 barrels of oil at a price of $70 per barrel on a specific date in the future. The contract will also specify the quality of the oil, such as the API gravity and sulfur content.

One of the key advantages of futures trading is leverage. Because futures contracts require only a small fraction of the underlying asset's value as a margin, investors can control a large amount of the asset with a relatively small investment. This leverage can amplify both gains and losses, so futures trading involves a high degree of risk.

Futures contracts can be used for both speculative and hedging purposes. Speculators use futures contracts to bet on the future direction of prices, hoping to profit from price fluctuations. Hedgers use futures contracts to lock in a price for a commodity or financial instrument, reducing their exposure to price volatility.

Futures trading is typically done through a broker, who acts as an intermediary between the buyer and seller of the contract. The broker charges a commission for their services, as well as other fees and expenses associated with trading futures.

One of the unique features of futures trading is that contracts are marked-to-market on a daily basis. This means that the gains and losses on the contract are settled on a daily basis, with the profits or losses being added or subtracted from the investor's account balance. This daily settlement process helps to minimize the risk of default by either party to the contract.

Overall, futures trading can be a useful tool for investors looking to speculate on the future price of commodities or financial instruments, as well as for hedgers looking to manage their exposure to price volatility. However, futures trading involves a high degree of risk and requires specialized knowledge and expertise. Investors should carefully consider their investment objectives, risk tolerance, and the costs associated with futures trading before investing in this market.

Part 2: Interest in Investing

In finance, interest is the cost of borrowing money or the return on invested capital. Interest can be calculated as a percentage of the principal amount borrowed or invested, and is usually expressed as an annual percentage rate (APR).

When you invest money, you may earn interest on your investment. This is a return on your investment that is paid to you by the issuer of the investment instrument, such as a bond or savings account. The interest rate on an investment also depends on several factors, including the issuer's creditworthiness, the length of the investment term, and market conditions.

Interest rates are an important aspect of finance because they affect the cost of borrowing and the return on investment. They can also impact the overall health of the economy. For example, low interest rates can stimulate economic growth by encouraging borrowing and spending, while high interest rates can slow down economic growth by making borrowing more expensive.

Earning interest refers to the return or profit earned on an investment over a certain period of time. When you deposit money into an interest-bearing account, such as a savings account, you are essentially lending your money to the bank or financial institution. In return, the bank pays you interest on your deposit.

The interest rate on your deposit is usually determined by several factors, such as the current market conditions, the type of account, the length of the investment term, and the amount of money you are depositing. Interest rates can be fixed, meaning they stay the same for the entire investment term, or variable, meaning they can change over time based on market conditions.

The interest you earn on your deposit is usually calculated using an annual percentage rate (APR), which is the percentage of your balance that the bank pays you as interest over a year. For example, if you have

$10,000 deposited in a savings account with a 2% APR, you would earn $200 in interest over the course of a year.

The amount of interest you earn on your deposit can also be compounded, which means that the interest is added to your account balance and then earns interest on that new balance. Compounding can increase your total return on investment over time, especially if you are able to keep your money in the account for a long period of time.

Overall, earning interest is a way to generate passive income from your savings or investments. It can be a relatively low-risk way to earn a return on your money, but it is important to consider the interest rate, fees, and other factors when choosing an interest-bearing account or investment.

Interest rates are the cost of borrowing or the return on lending money. They are typically expressed as a percentage of the principal amount and are charged or earned over a specific period of time, usually on an annual basis. Interest rates are an important tool used by central banks to influence the economy by affecting the cost of borrowing, spending, and investment.

Interest rates can be classified into several categories based on the type of interest rate, the length of the loan term, and the method of calculation. Some common types of interest rates include:

1. Fixed interest rates: These are interest rates that remain the same over the entire length of the loan or investment term. Fixed interest rates are commonly used in mortgages, personal loans, and bonds.

2. Variable interest rates: These are interest rates that fluctuate over time based on market conditions. Variable interest rates are commonly used in adjustable-rate mortgages, credit cards, and some types of savings accounts.

3. Prime interest rates: These are the interest rates that commercial banks charge their most creditworthy customers. The prime rate is usually used as a benchmark for other types of loans and interest rates.

4. Federal funds rate: This is the interest rate at which commercial banks lend to each other overnight to meet their reserve requirements. The Federal Reserve Bank uses the federal funds rate as a tool to influence the economy by adjusting the money supply and controlling inflation.

5. Annual percentage rate (APR): This is the total cost of borrowing, including both the interest rate and any fees associated with the loan. The APR is used to compare the cost of different types of loans and credit cards.

Interest rates can have a significant impact on the economy, affecting consumer spending, business investment, and inflation. When interest rates are low, borrowing becomes cheaper, which can stimulate spending and investment. However, low interest rates can also lead to inflation and asset bubbles. Conversely, high interest rates can slow down economic growth and borrowing, but can also help control inflation. The balance of interest rates is an important factor in macroeconomic policy and financial decision-making.

The typical APR (Annual Percentage Rate) for earning interest and regular interest rates can vary depending on the type of account, investment, or loan you are considering, as well as market conditions, economic factors, and the issuer's creditworthiness.

For earning interest, the APR can vary widely depending on the type of account and financial institution. For example, a high-yield savings account may offer an APR of 1.50% or more, while a traditional savings account may offer an APR of 0.10% or less. Certificates of deposit (CDs) typically offer higher interest rates than savings accounts, with rates ranging from 0.50% to 2.50% or more, depending on the term length and the issuer.

It's important to note that interest rates can change over time based on a variety of factors, so it's always a good idea to compare rates from multiple issuers and shop around for the best deal. Additionally, the APR is just one factor to consider when evaluating a financial product - other factors like fees, penalties, and repayment terms should also be taken into account.

Interest rates can be encountered in many different areas of personal finance and investing. Some common places where someone might encounter interest rates include:

1. Savings accounts: When you deposit money into a savings account, the bank or financial institution may pay you interest on your balance.

2. Certificates of deposit (CDs): CDs are a type of investment that allows you to earn interest on your deposit over a fixed period of time.

3. Bonds: Bonds are a type of fixed-income investment that pays interest to investors over the life of the bond.

4. Mortgages: When you take out a mortgage to buy a home, you will be charged interest on the amount you borrow.

5. Auto loans: If you finance a car purchase, you will be charged interest on the loan amount.

6. Credit cards: Credit cards charge interest on balances that are not paid in full by the due date.

7. Personal loans: If you take out a personal loan, you will be charged interest on the loan amount.

8. Student loans: Student loans charge interest on the amount borrowed to finance education expenses.

In addition to these specific financial products, interest rates can also be encountered in the broader economy, such as the interest rates set by central banks, which can influence the cost of borrowing and spending for businesses and individuals alike.

While interest rates can be a useful tool for managing personal finances and investing, there are also several pitfalls and risks associated with them that individuals should be aware of. Some of these pitfalls include:

1. High-interest rates can lead to debt: When interest rates are high, borrowing money becomes more expensive, and individuals may be more likely to take on debt that they are unable to repay.

2. Variable interest rates can be unpredictable: When interest rates are variable, they can be difficult to predict, which can make it challenging for borrowers and investors to plan for the future.

3. Low-interest rates can hurt savings: When interest rates are low, the returns on savings accounts, CDs, and other types of investments may not keep up with inflation, which can erode the value of savings over time.

4. Interest rates can be influenced by external factors: Interest rates can be affected by a variety of external factors, including changes in the economy, monetary policy decisions by central banks, and geopolitical events, which can be difficult to predict.

5. Interest rates can be subject to fees and penalties: In addition to the interest charged on loans and other types of credit, borrowers may also be subject to fees and penalties for late payments,

missed payments, or other types of default, which can increase the cost of borrowing.

6. Interest rates can be used to manipulate financial markets: In some cases, interest rates may be used to manipulate financial markets, which can create a volatile and unpredictable environment for investors and borrowers alike.

In general, it is important for individuals to carefully consider the risks and benefits of interest rates before making any financial decisions. By understanding how interest rates work and the potential pitfalls associated with them, individuals can make more informed decisions about their personal finances and investments.

Part 3: Positive Collections

In finance, a positive collection refers to a group of financial assets that have been selected because they have a positive expected return. These assets could include stocks, bonds, real estate, or other investments. The term is often used in contrast to a "negative" collection, which would consist of financial assets that have a negative expected return or are seen as risky.

For example, a positive collection of stocks might include companies that are expected to perform well in the future, such as those with strong financials, good management teams, and a history of growth. A negative collection of stocks, on the other hand, might include companies that are struggling financially, have poor management, or are facing headwinds in their industry.

In terms of portfolio management, positive collections are often used as a way to identify the most promising investments and create a diversified portfolio that maximizes returns while minimizing risk. This is often done through the use of screening tools and investment strategies that focus on specific characteristics of the assets, such as strong fundamentals, low volatility, or high dividend yields.

In addition, positive collections can also be used in the field of credit risk management, where the positive collection refers to the good credit borrowers or clients that have a good credit history and are expected to repay their debt.

Overall, in finance, a positive collection refers to a group of financial assets that have been selected because they have a positive expected return and are seen as less risky, while a negative collection would be the opposite.

There are many different types of companies that could be considered to have positive collections. Some examples include:

1. Blue chip companies: These are large, well-established companies with strong financials, a history of steady growth, and a reputation for stability and reliability. Examples include companies like Coca-Cola, IBM, and Johnson & Johnson.

2. Growth companies: These are companies that are expected to experience strong growth in the future, typically due to new products, services, or emerging markets. Examples include companies like Amazon, Netflix, and Tesla.
3. Dividend-paying companies: These are companies that have a history of paying dividends to shareholders, which can provide a steady stream of income for investors. Examples include companies like AT&T, Procter & Gamble, and Wal-Mart.
4. Low Volatility Companies: These companies have a low volatility in their stock prices, providing a more stable return for investors. Examples include companies like consumer staples, utilities or real estate companies.
5. Companies in defensive industries: These are companies that operate in industries that are less affected by economic downturns, such as consumer staples and healthcare. Examples include companies like Nestle, Johnson & Johnson, and Procter & Gamble.
6. Companies with strong brand reputation: These are companies with a strong reputation and brand, which can help to attract customers and build customer loyalty. Examples include companies like Apple, Nike, and Coca-Cola.

It's important to note that these are just a few examples and the characteristics that make a company positive collection may change over time and vary depending on the market conditions and industry.

Blue Chip Companies

Blue chip companies are large, well-established companies that have a strong financial performance, a long track record of steady growth, and a reputation for stability and reliability. These companies are considered to be among the most financially secure and profitable in their respective industries. They are considered to be part of the positive collection in the stock market.

Some of the characteristics that can define a blue chip company include:

- Strong financials: Blue chip companies typically have a strong balance sheet, with high levels of liquidity and low levels of debt. This makes them well-positioned to weather economic downturns and continue to grow over the long-term.

- History of steady growth: Blue chip companies have a long track record of steady growth in terms of revenue, earnings, and market share. This can provide investors with a sense of security that the company will continue to perform well in the future.
- Diversified revenue streams: Blue chip companies often have diversified revenue streams, which can help to mitigate risk in case one particular business unit or product experiences a downturn.
- Brand reputation: Blue chip companies often have a strong reputation and brand, which can help to attract customers and build customer loyalty.

Examples of blue chip companies include: Coca-Cola, IBM, Johnson & Johnson, Procter & Gamble, McDonald's, and Wal-Mart. These companies are considered to be among the most financially secure and profitable in their respective industries and are often included in stock market indices such as the S&P 500 and the Dow Jones Industrial Average.

It's important to note that while blue chip companies are generally considered to be safe investments, they are not immune to market fluctuations, and their stock prices can still be affected by economic downturns or changes in the industry.

Dividend-Paying Companies

Dividend-paying companies are companies that have a history of paying dividends to shareholders, which can provide a steady stream of income for investors. Dividends are a portion of a company's profits that are distributed to shareholders on a regular basis, usually quarterly. Dividend-paying companies are considered to be part of the positive collection in the stock market.

Some of the characteristics that can define a dividend-paying company include:

- Strong financials: In order to pay dividends, a company must have a strong financial performance and enough cash flow to cover the dividends.
- History of paying dividends: Dividend-paying companies have a history of paying dividends to shareholders over a period of time.

- Consistency in the dividend payments: Dividend-paying companies tend to have a consistent dividend payment history, and they are less likely to cut dividends.
- Diversified revenue streams: Dividend-paying companies often have diversified revenue streams, which can help to mitigate risk in case one particular business unit or product experiences a downturn.

Examples of dividend-paying companies include: AT&T, Procter & Gamble, Wal-Mart, Johnson & Johnson, and Coca-Cola. These companies are considered to be among the most financially secure and profitable in their respective industries and are often included in stock market indices such as the S&P 500 and the Dow Jones Industrial Average.

It's important to note that while dividend-paying companies are generally considered to be safe investments, they are not immune to market fluctuations, and their stock prices can still be affected by economic downturns or changes in the industry. Additionally, dividends are not guaranteed and the company can change or stop paying dividends in the future.

Part 4: Cryptocurrency

Cryptocurrency is a digital or virtual currency that uses cryptography for security and operates independently of a central bank. Cryptocurrencies utilize blockchain technology, which is a decentralized ledger that records all transactions in a transparent and immutable way.

Unlike traditional currencies, which are backed by governments or other financial institutions, cryptocurrencies rely on complex algorithms and cryptographic techniques to ensure the integrity and security of their transactions. They are also not subject to government regulation, which allows for greater anonymity and decentralization.

The most well-known cryptocurrency is Bitcoin, which was created in 2009 by an anonymous person or group using the pseudonym Satoshi Nakamoto. Since then, thousands of other cryptocurrencies have emerged, including Ethereum, Litecoin, and Ripple, among others.

Cryptocurrencies are typically bought and sold on cryptocurrency exchanges, where users can trade one cryptocurrency for another or exchange cryptocurrency for traditional fiat currencies like the US dollar or euro. Cryptocurrencies can also be used to purchase goods and services from merchants who accept them as payment.

Despite their potential benefits, such as increased security, privacy, and accessibility, cryptocurrencies also face significant challenges, including market volatility, security risks, and regulatory uncertainty. As a result, investors and businesses considering cryptocurrencies should carefully evaluate their potential risks and benefits before making any investments or transactions.

Some popular cryptocurrencies include:

1. Bitcoin (BTC) - Considered the first and most popular cryptocurrency, Bitcoin is valued at over $40,000 per coin as of September 2021.

2. Ethereum (ETH) - Ethereum is the second-largest cryptocurrency by market capitalization and is valued at over $3,000 per coin as of September 2021.

3. Binance Coin (BNB) - Binance Coin is the native token of the Binance exchange and is valued at over $300 per coin as of September 2021.

4. Cardano (ADA) - Cardano is a third-generation cryptocurrency that aims to solve scalability and sustainability issues. It is valued at over $2 per coin as of September 2021.

5. Dogecoin (DOGE) - Dogecoin is a meme-based cryptocurrency that was created as a joke but gained a cult following. It is valued at over $0.20 per coin as of September 2021.

6. XRP (XRP) - XRP is a cryptocurrency that was created by the fintech company Ripple and is valued at over $1 per coin as of September 2021.

7. Solana (SOL) - Solana is a fast and scalable blockchain platform that supports decentralized applications. It is valued at over $150 per coin as of September 2021.

8. Polkadot (DOT) - Polkadot is a blockchain platform that aims to enable interoperability between different blockchains. It is valued at over $30 per coin as of September 2021.

9. Chainlink (LINK) - Chainlink is a decentralized oracle network that connects smart contracts to external data sources. It is valued at over $30 per coin as of September 2021.

10. Litecoin (LTC) - Litecoin is a peer-to-peer cryptocurrency that was created as a faster and more scalable alternative to Bitcoin. It is valued at over $150 per coin as of September 2021.

Investing in cryptocurrency, like any investment, carries inherent risks and uncertainties. Cryptocurrencies are known for their volatility, and their value can fluctuate rapidly in a short amount of time. It is also important to note that the cryptocurrency market is still relatively new and largely unregulated, which adds to the uncertainty.

While some investors have profited significantly from investing in cryptocurrency, others have experienced significant losses. As with any investment, it is important to do your own research, understand the risks involved, and make an informed decision based on your financial goals, risk tolerance, and investment strategy. It is also recommended to consult with a financial advisor before making any investment decisions.

Ultimately, whether investing in cryptocurrency is financially sound or not depends on a variety of factors, including market conditions, global economic trends, and individual investment goals and risk tolerance.

Getting started with cryptocurrency can seem daunting, but it is relatively straightforward. Here are some basic steps to help you get started:

1. Choose a cryptocurrency exchange: The first step is to choose a reputable cryptocurrency exchange that supports the cryptocurrencies you want to buy. Examples of popular exchanges include Coinbase, Binance, and Kraken.

2. Create an account: Once you have selected an exchange, create an account by providing your personal information and completing the verification process, which typically involves uploading a government-issued ID and a proof of address.

3. Fund your account: Next, you will need to fund your account by depositing funds using a bank transfer or a credit/debit card.

4. Buy cryptocurrency: Once you have funded your account, you can buy cryptocurrency by selecting the cryptocurrency you want to purchase and specifying the amount you want to spend.

5. Store your cryptocurrency: After you have purchased
    cryptocurrency, you can store it in a digital wallet. A wallet is a
    secure digital storage solution for your cryptocurrency. Examples
    of popular wallets include Ledger, Trezor, and MetaMask.

It is important to note that investing in cryptocurrency carries risks and
uncertainties, and it is important to do your own research, understand the
risks involved, and make an informed decision based on your financial
goals, risk tolerance, and investment strategy. It is also recommended to
consult with a financial advisor before making any investment decisions.

Part 5: AI

Artificial Intelligence (AI) refers to the development of computer systems that can perform tasks that typically require human intelligence, such as visual perception, speech recognition, decision-making, and language translation. AI systems use algorithms and mathematical models to analyze data, learn from patterns, and make predictions or decisions based on that data.

AI is a broad field that encompasses many sub-disciplines, including machine learning, natural language processing, computer vision, robotics, and cognitive computing. These different areas of AI are designed to solve different problems and achieve different goals.

Machine learning is perhaps the most well-known sub-discipline of AI, which involves training computer systems to recognize patterns in data, and to make predictions or decisions based on those patterns. This is achieved through the use of algorithms that are trained on large amounts of data, and can be adapted or improved over time as more data becomes available.

Natural language processing (NLP) is another important area of AI, which involves teaching computers to understand and respond to human language. NLP is used in applications such as chatbots, voice assistants, and automated translation systems.

Computer vision is another sub-discipline of AI that focuses on enabling machines to interpret and understand visual information, such as images and videos. This is used in applications such as facial recognition, object detection, and self-driving cars.

Overall, AI is a rapidly growing field with significant potential to transform many aspects of our lives, from healthcare and education to transportation and entertainment.

AI has a wide range of uses across many different industries and sectors, including healthcare, finance, manufacturing, retail, transportation, and entertainment. Here are some of the most common uses of AI:

1. Automation: AI is used to automate repetitive or mundane tasks, such as data entry, processing, and analysis. This helps to improve efficiency and reduce errors, allowing human workers to focus on more complex or creative tasks.

2. Personalization: AI is used to personalize customer experiences, such as recommending products or services based on past behavior or preferences. This helps to improve customer satisfaction and loyalty.

3. Decision-making: AI is used to make better and faster decisions, based on data and patterns. This is particularly useful in areas such as finance and healthcare, where decisions can have significant consequences.

4. Predictive maintenance: AI is used to predict when equipment or machinery is likely to fail, allowing for preventive maintenance to be carried out before the problem occurs. This helps to reduce downtime and maintenance costs.

5. Medical diagnosis and treatment: AI is used to analyze medical data, such as X-rays and medical images, to help with diagnosis and treatment decisions. This helps to improve accuracy and speed up the diagnosis process.

6. Fraud detection: AI is used to detect and prevent fraud, such as in credit card transactions or insurance claims. This helps to reduce losses and protect against fraudulent activity.

7. Autonomous systems: AI is used to power autonomous systems, such as self-driving cars and drones. This allows for greater efficiency, safety, and accuracy in these systems.

8. Natural language processing: AI is used to analyze and respond to human language, allowing for applications such as voice assistants and chatbots.

Overall, AI has the potential to transform many aspects of our lives, from improving efficiency and accuracy in our work to enhancing the way we interact with technology and each other.

While AI has many benefits, there are also potential pitfalls that need to be considered. Here are some of the main pitfalls of AI:

1. Bias: AI systems are only as good as the data they are trained on, and if the data is biased or incomplete, then the AI system may produce biased or incomplete results. This can have serious consequences, particularly in areas such as criminal justice or hiring decisions.
2. Job displacement: As AI systems become more advanced, they have the potential to replace human workers in certain tasks or industries. This could lead to job displacement and a widening income gap.
3. Privacy concerns: AI systems often require access to large amounts of data in order to learn and improve. This can raise privacy concerns, particularly if the data includes sensitive information such as health records or personal financial information.
4. Security risks: AI systems can also be vulnerable to security breaches, which could lead to sensitive data being accessed or manipulated.
5. Lack of transparency: AI systems can be difficult to understand or interpret, particularly if they use complex algorithms or machine

learning techniques. This lack of transparency can make it difficult to identify and address any biases or errors in the system.

6. Overreliance on technology: AI systems are not infallible, and if people become too reliant on them, it could lead to complacency or a lack of critical thinking skills.

Overall, it is important to approach the development and deployment of AI systems with caution, and to address any potential pitfalls or risks in a thoughtful and proactive manner. This can help to ensure that the benefits of AI are maximized while minimizing any negative consequences.

AI has many uses in the finance industry, where it is used to improve efficiency, accuracy, and customer experiences. Here are some of the main uses of AI in finance:

1. Fraud detection: AI is used to detect and prevent fraud, particularly in areas such as credit card transactions or insurance claims. AI algorithms can quickly analyze large amounts of data to identify any suspicious activity and alert financial institutions to potential fraud.

2. Investment analysis: AI is used to analyze and predict market trends, allowing financial institutions to make more informed investment decisions. This can include analyzing past market data, news articles, and social media feeds to identify potential investment opportunities.

3. Risk management: AI is used to manage risk in financial transactions and investments. AI algorithms can quickly analyze risk factors such as credit scores, loan history, and market trends to determine the likelihood of default or other risks.

4. Customer service: AI is used to improve customer service in finance, particularly through the use of chatbots and virtual assistants. This allows customers to quickly and easily access information about their accounts or financial products.

5. Personalized recommendations: AI is used to provide personalized financial advice and recommendations to customers. This can include recommending investment options or financial products based on the customer's past behavior and preferences.

6. Regulatory compliance: AI is used to ensure compliance with regulatory requirements in finance, particularly in areas such as anti-money laundering and know-your-customer regulations. AI algorithms can quickly analyze large amounts of data to identify any potential compliance issues.

Overall, AI has the potential to transform many aspects of the finance industry, from improving efficiency and accuracy to enhancing customer experiences and reducing fraud.

Yes, someone could potentially use AI to manage their personal finances. There are already many AI-powered tools and apps available that can help individuals manage their finances more effectively. These tools can provide a range of features, such as budgeting assistance, investment advice, and personalized recommendations.

Here are some ways in which AI can be used to manage personal finances:

1. Budgeting: AI-powered budgeting tools can analyze spending habits and income to help individuals create a personalized budget. These tools can also provide alerts and reminders to help individuals stay on track with their budget.

2. Investment advice: AI-powered investment platforms can analyze market trends and risk factors to provide personalized investment advice. These platforms can also monitor portfolios and make adjustments based on market conditions.

3. Credit score monitoring: AI-powered credit score monitoring tools can provide real-time updates on credit scores and alerts for any changes or potential fraud.

4. Personalized recommendations: AI-powered personal finance apps can provide personalized recommendations for financial products such as credit cards, loans, and savings accounts based on an individual's past behavior and preferences.

5. Expense tracking: AI-powered expense tracking tools can automatically categorize expenses and provide insights into spending patterns. This can help individuals identify areas where they can cut back on spending and save money.

Overall, AI can be a powerful tool for managing personal finances, providing personalized recommendations and insights that can help individuals make more informed financial decisions.

Investing in AI (artificial intelligence) can potentially be a good idea, as AI is a rapidly growing and evolving field that is transforming many industries. AI has the potential to improve efficiency, productivity, and decision-making across a range of sectors, including healthcare, finance, manufacturing, and transportation.

There are several ways to invest in AI, including purchasing individual stocks of companies that are involved in AI development, investing in AI-focused mutual funds or ETFs, or investing in startups that are developing innovative AI solutions.

However, it's important to keep in mind that investing in AI is not without risks. As with any investment, there is no guarantee of a return, and AI companies may face challenges such as regulatory hurdles, technological barriers, or competition from other players in the market. It's important to conduct thorough research, assess the risks and potential rewards, and invest with a long-term perspective in mind.

Additionally, investing in AI requires specialized knowledge and expertise, so it may not be suitable for all investors. Before making any investment decisions, it's important to consult with a financial advisor and carefully consider your investment objectives, risk tolerance, and financial situation.

Part 6: NFTs

NFTs (Non-Fungible Tokens) are digital assets that represent ownership of unique items such as artwork, music, videos, or other digital content. Unlike cryptocurrencies such as Bitcoin or Ethereum, which are fungible, meaning one unit can be exchanged for another identical unit, each NFT is unique and represents a specific digital asset.

NFTs are created using blockchain technology, which allows for the creation of a decentralized digital ledger that records the ownership and transaction history of each NFT. This makes it possible to verify the authenticity and ownership of each digital asset represented by an NFT.

NFTs have gained popularity in the art world as a way for artists to sell their work directly to collectors without the need for intermediaries such as galleries or auction houses. They have also been used in the music industry to represent ownership of digital music files or streaming rights.

The value of an NFT is determined by various factors such as the rarity of the digital asset, the popularity of the creator, and the demand from collectors. Some NFTs have sold for millions of dollars, making them a potentially lucrative investment opportunity.

However, there are also concerns about the environmental impact of NFTs due to the significant energy consumption required by blockchain technology. Additionally, there are concerns about the potential for fraud and the lack of regulation in the NFT market.

To create an NFT, you will need to follow these basic steps:

1. Choose a blockchain: NFTs are created using blockchain technology, so you will need to choose a blockchain that supports NFTs. Ethereum is currently the most popular blockchain for creating NFTs.

2. Create a digital asset: You will need to create a unique digital asset that you want to represent with an NFT. This could be artwork, music, video, or any other digital content.

3. Mint the NFT: Once you have created the digital asset, you will need to use a software platform or service that allows you to mint the NFT. Minting an NFT involves registering the digital asset on the chosen blockchain and creating a unique token that represents ownership of the asset. This process typically involves setting parameters such as the name of the NFT, the total supply of the NFT, and the royalty fee that the creator will receive for future resales.

4. List the NFT for sale: After minting the NFT, you can list it for sale on a marketplace that specializes in NFTs, such as OpenSea, Rarible, or SuperRare. Alternatively, you can sell the NFT privately or through an auction.

5. Transfer ownership: Once the NFT is sold, the ownership of the digital asset represented by the NFT is transferred to the buyer. The transaction is recorded on the blockchain and can be verified by anyone.

It is important to note that the process of creating an NFT can be complex, and there are several factors to consider such as the cost of minting the NFT, the gas fees associated with using the blockchain, and the legal implications of selling digital assets. As such, it is recommended that you seek professional advice before creating and selling NFTs.

The popularity of NFTs can fluctuate quickly, and it can be challenging to identify the most popular ones at any given time. However, some NFTs have gained significant attention and value in recent months. Here are a few examples:

1. CryptoPunks: CryptoPunks are a collection of 10,000 unique 8-bit characters, each with its own distinct features and traits. They were one of the first NFT projects on Ethereum and have become highly sought after. In March 2021, a single CryptoPunk sold for a record-breaking $69 million.

2. Bored Ape Yacht Club: Bored Ape Yacht Club (BAYC) is a collection of 10,000 unique hand-drawn ape NFTs. Each BAYC NFT gives the owner access to a private online community, and the project has gained a significant following since its launch in April 2021.

3. Art Blocks: Art Blocks is a generative art project that creates unique NFTs using algorithms. Each NFT is generated on demand and is one of a kind. The project has gained popularity for its ability to create highly intricate and visually stunning art pieces.

4. NBA Top Shot: NBA Top Shot is an NFT project that allows users to collect and trade digital basketball highlights. Each highlight is represented by a unique NFT, and the project has become popular among basketball fans and collectors.

5. Pudgy Penguins: Pudgy Penguins is a collection of 8,888 unique hand-drawn penguin NFTs. The project has gained popularity for its cute and quirky art style, and some Pudgy Penguins have sold for significant amounts.

It is worth noting that the NFT market is highly volatile, and the popularity and value of NFTs can fluctuate rapidly. Additionally, new

NFT projects and collections are being created all the time, so this list may quickly become outdated.

Investing in NFTs can offer several potential benefits, although it is worth noting that it also carries risks, and investment decisions should be made after careful consideration and consultation with professional advisors. Here are some potential benefits of investing in NFTs:

1. Potential for high returns: Some NFTs have sold for millions of dollars, offering the potential for high returns on investment.

2. Access to unique and exclusive assets: NFTs represent ownership of unique and exclusive digital assets that cannot be replicated or duplicated, making them highly valuable to collectors and fans.

3. Opportunities for creators: NFTs can provide opportunities for artists, musicians, and other creators to sell their work directly to fans and collectors, without the need for intermediaries such as galleries or record labels.

4. Accessible market: The NFT market is accessible to anyone with an internet connection, which means that investors from around the world can participate in it.

5. Transparency and authenticity: NFTs are created using blockchain technology, which provides a transparent and secure record of ownership and transaction history. This can help to prevent fraud and ensure the authenticity of the assets represented by NFTs.

It is important to note that investing in NFTs carries risks, including market volatility, lack of regulation, and the potential for fraudulent activities. Additionally, the value of NFTs can be highly speculative and may not reflect the underlying value of the digital assets they represent. Therefore, it is essential to conduct thorough research and seek professional advice before investing in NFTs.

NFTs have gained significant attention in recent months, but like any new technology or investment opportunity, there are potential pitfalls that investors and collectors should be aware of. Here are some of the most significant pitfalls of NFTs:

1. High volatility: The value of NFTs can be highly volatile and can fluctuate rapidly, making it challenging to predict their long-term value.

2. Lack of regulation: The NFT market is largely unregulated, which means that investors may not have the same protections and guarantees as they would with regulated investments.

3. Environmental concerns: The process of minting and trading NFTs consumes a significant amount of energy, which has raised concerns about the environmental impact of the technology.

4. Lack of underlying value: The value of some NFTs may be driven more by speculation and hype than the underlying value of the digital assets they represent.

5. Lack of liquidity: NFTs can be challenging to sell or trade quickly, which means that investors may have difficulty converting their NFT holdings into cash if they need to do so quickly.

6. Legal risks: There are potential legal risks associated with creating and selling NFTs, including copyright infringement and intellectual property disputes.

7. Hype and scams: The hype surrounding NFTs has attracted the attention of scammers and fraudsters, who may try to take advantage of inexperienced investors or collectors.

It is essential to do thorough research and seek professional advice before investing in NFTs. While NFTs can offer significant opportunities, they also carry risks, and it is essential to approach them with caution and a clear understanding of the potential pitfalls.

There are several ways to obtain an NFT, and the process may vary depending on the NFT project and platform. Here are some common ways to obtain an NFT:

1. Purchase from a marketplace: The most common way to obtain an NFT is to purchase it from a marketplace. There are several NFT marketplaces available, such as OpenSea, Rarible, and SuperRare, where you can browse and purchase NFTs from various collections.

2. Participate in a sale or auction: Some NFTs are sold through auctions or sales, where the highest bidder or buyer can obtain the NFT. These events are often promoted through social media or email newsletters and can be an opportunity to obtain a rare or highly sought-after NFT.

3. Mint your own NFT: If you are an artist or creator, you can mint your own NFT using one of the many platforms that offer NFT minting services. These platforms typically require you to upload your digital asset and then issue a new NFT that represents ownership of that asset.

4. Receive as a gift or reward: NFTs can also be gifted or awarded as a reward for participating in a community or project. For example, some NFT projects may offer NFTs to users who contribute to their development or participate in their social media channels.

Once you have obtained an NFT, you will typically receive a unique digital wallet address that represents ownership of the NFT on the blockchain. You can then view and manage your NFT collection through your digital wallet, which may be a software or hardware wallet that supports the specific blockchain that the NFT is issued on.

Chapter 7: Moving toward the Path to Financial Success

Banking: The Foundation of Financial Literacy

Banking is the cornerstone of financial management, providing essential services that allow individuals and businesses to manage money effectively. Understanding the basics of banking enables individuals to make informed decisions about their finances.

Basics of Banking

Banks serve as financial intermediaries that facilitate transactions, offer savings and investment opportunities, and provide loans. Understanding how banks function is key to making strategic financial choices.

Aspects of Banking

- **Deposit Accounts:** Savings accounts, checking accounts, and certificates of deposit (CDs) offer varying levels of liquidity and interest rates.
- **Lending Services:** Banks provide loans, mortgages, and credit lines that help individuals and businesses achieve financial goals.
- **Financial Security:** Banks safeguard funds and offer fraud protection, enhancing financial stability.

Types of Accounts

- **Checking Accounts:** Designed for everyday transactions with easy access via debit cards and checks.
- **Savings Accounts:** Provide interest on deposits, helping individuals grow their wealth.
- **Money Market Accounts:** A hybrid between savings and checking accounts, offering higher interest rates with limited transactions.

- **Certificates of Deposit (CDs):** Fixed-term deposits with higher interest rates, suitable for long-term savings.

Currency and Its Types

Currency serves as a medium of exchange, facilitating trade and commerce. Various forms of currency include:

- **Fiat Currency:** Issued by governments and not backed by a physical commodity.
- **Digital Currency:** Includes cryptocurrencies like Bitcoin and Ethereum, which operate on decentralized networks.
- **Foreign Exchange (Forex):** The global marketplace for trading different national currencies.

Bankruptcy: Navigating Financial Hardships

Bankruptcy is a legal process designed to help individuals and businesses manage overwhelming debt. Understanding its implications is crucial to financial recovery.

Individual Bankruptcy

- **Chapter 7 Bankruptcy:** Involves liquidating assets to pay off creditors.
- **Chapter 13 Bankruptcy:** Allows individuals to restructure debt and create a repayment plan.

Business Bankruptcy

- **Chapter 11 Bankruptcy:** Enables businesses to reorganize debts while continuing operations.
- **Chapter 7 Business Bankruptcy:** Results in the liquidation of assets to pay creditors, often leading to business closure.

Debt Relief and Credit Management

- **Debt Consolidation:** Combining multiple debts into a single loan with lower interest rates.

- **Credit Counseling:** Professional services that assist in budgeting and repayment strategies.
- **Credit Reporting and Repair:** Maintaining a good credit score is essential for financial opportunities. Regularly reviewing credit reports and disputing inaccuracies can improve credit standing.

Insurance: Protecting Your Assets and Future

Insurance provides financial security against unexpected losses, ensuring long-term stability.

Types of Insurance

- **Health Insurance:** Covers medical expenses, reducing out-of-pocket costs.
- **Auto Insurance:** Protects against vehicle-related accidents and damages.
- **Homeowners Insurance:** Provides coverage for property damage and liability.
- **Life Insurance:** Ensures financial protection for dependents in case of the policyholder's death.

Healthcare and VA Benefits

Healthcare coverage varies by provider, employer, and government assistance programs. Veterans Affairs (VA) benefits offer specialized coverage for former military personnel, including healthcare, disability compensation, and educational assistance.

Loans: Accessing Financial Resources

Loans provide the necessary funds for major expenses but must be managed responsibly.

Types of Loans and Their Uses

- **Personal Loans:** Used for various expenses, including debt consolidation and emergency expenses.

- **Mortgage Loans:** Enable homeownership by financing property purchases.
- **Student Loans:** Support educational endeavors, with repayment plans available post-graduation.
- **Business Loans:** Assist entrepreneurs in starting and expanding their ventures.

Understanding Interest Rates

Interest is the cost of borrowing money, and its rates vary based on creditworthiness and loan type. Fixed rates remain constant, while variable rates fluctuate with market conditions.

Investing: Growing Wealth for the Future

Investing is a strategic way to build wealth and secure financial stability.

Types of Investments

- **Stocks:** Shares of a company that provide ownership and potential dividends.
- **Bonds:** Debt securities issued by governments or corporations with fixed interest returns.
- **Real Estate:** Investing in property for rental income or resale value.
- **Mutual Funds:** Pooled investments managed by professionals, offering diversified portfolios.

Emerging Investment Trends

- **Cryptocurrency:** Digital assets that leverage blockchain technology for decentralized transactions.
- **Artificial Intelligence (AI) Investments:** Companies utilizing AI technology for innovation and efficiency.
- **Non-Fungible Tokens (NFTs):** Digital assets representing unique items such as art, music, and collectibles.
- **Positive Collections:** Investments focused on socially responsible companies and sustainable practices.

Conclusion: Take Control of Your Financial Future

Understanding financial principles empowers individuals to make informed decisions and secure their future. By mastering banking fundamentals, managing debt responsibly, utilizing insurance for protection, leveraging loans wisely, and exploring investment opportunities, individuals can achieve long-term financial success.

Moving Forward

Financial literacy is a lifelong journey. Continue to educate yourself, seek expert advice when needed, and practice disciplined financial habits. Take advantage of financial literacy courses, online resources, and mentorship opportunities to expand your knowledge. By applying these principles, you can confidently navigate the financial world and achieve lasting prosperity.

About the Author

Dan Kost is a dedicated financial strategist, educator, entrepreneur, and the CEO of Dakdan Worldwide, a global media holding company specializing in consulting and marketing. With decades of experience in finance, business management, and career development, he has guided countless individuals toward making informed financial decisions that lead to long-term prosperity.

Dan published his first book in 1982, *The First Book About Credit Repair*, and played a key role in the development of the Consumer Credit Services Act, which now protects consumers nationwide by ensuring their rights to safeguard and repair their credit. He also founded the National Association of Credit Counselors, which grew to 3,500 members before he passed on its leadership. Throughout his career, he has worked across multiple sectors, including bankruptcy, insurance, securities, financial consulting, corporate finance, real estate, and business development, giving him a well-rounded perspective on financial literacy and economic empowerment.

As the founder and CEO of Dakdan Worldwide, Dan has been instrumental in helping businesses and individuals achieve success through strategic marketing, financial planning, and innovative business solutions. Under his leadership, Dakdan Worldwide has expanded its reach, assisting clients across various industries with growth strategies, branding, and financial management. His extensive experience in global business operations provides him with unique insights into financial trends, market dynamics, and economic strategies that benefit both businesses and individuals.

Beyond his professional accomplishments, Dan is deeply committed to financial literacy education and empowerment. He has developed financial literacy programs, conducted workshops, and mentored individuals seeking to improve their financial well-being. His latest mission is to develop *Money Smarts*, an interactive game designed to teach financial literacy by guiding players through their entire financial journey. Recognizing the need for digital education in today's world, he aims to create an engaging, educational experience that helps children and young adults build strong financial habits from the moment they establish a banking relationship.

In the book *Money Smarts*, Dan combines his expertise and real-world experience to provide a comprehensive guide to financial literacy, money management, and career development. Through his work, he continues to inspire and educate readers, helping them navigate the complexities of finance with confidence and clarity.

Index:

About the Author: 178

Account balance alerts: 18

Alert Services and Finance: 18

AI in banking: 163

AI in lending: 163

AI in personal finance: 163

AI in risk management: 163

Aspects of Bank Accounts, Part 2: 13

Artificial Intelligence (AI): 162

Auto loans: 120, 232

Banking, Chapter 1: 7

Basics of Banking, Part 1: 7

Regulation of Banks: 7, 160

Risk management (by banks): 6, 160

Banking: The Foundation of Financial Literacy: 241

Bank Accounts: 13

Bankruptcy, Chapter 2: 36

Business Bankruptcy, Part 2: 45

Bankruptcy: Navigating Financial Hardships: 243

Comparing bankruptcy to defaulting: 49

Debt Relief, Part 4: 51

Individual Bankruptcy, Part 1: 40

Benefits of investing in NFTs: 170, 240

Bill payment alerts: 18

Blue Chip Companies: 155

Bonds: 141, 221

Budgeting: 16, 185

Bullion: 29, 179

Business expenses: 120, 210

Business Loans: 117

Car Loans: 119, 209, 232

Certificates of Deposit: 22, 175, 242

Chapter 11 Bankruptcy: 45

Checks: 31, 180

Coinage: 29

Commodity Investing: 248

Comparing bankruptcy to defaulting: 49

Completing loan entrance counseling: 117, 212, 215

Conclusion: Take Control of Your Financial Future: 249

Consolidating student loans: 120, 210

Cost of Money: 108, 202

Counterfeit Currency: 33, 182

Credit, Chapter 3: 55, 183

    Credit Building, Part 1: 56, 184

    Credit Card, Part 2: 58, 185

    Credit Inquiries: 61, 189

    Credit Reporting, Part 3: 61, 186, 245

    Credit Repair, Part 4: 65, 190, 245

    Credit Score: 62, 189

Credit Cards: 58, 161, 184, 203, 222, 230

Credit score alerts: 18

Cryptocurrency: 158, 226, 243, 248

Currencies, Part 4: 26, 177, 242

    Currency and Its Types: 242

    Types of currency: 28, 178, 242

Debt Consolidation: 244

Debt Relief: 51, 244

Defaulting, Part 3: 48

Dividend-Paying Companies: 156, 235

Earning more (to build bank account): 16, 165

Emergency expenses: 120

Exchange-Traded Funds (ETFs): 142, 226, 248

Fiat Currency: 30, 180, 242

Fixed interest rates: 131, 220, 247

Foreign Exchange (Forex): 243

Getting a non-federal student loan: 117, 212

Healthcare, Part 2: 89, 196

History of Currency: 26, 178

Home improvement: 120

How inflation affects a bank account: 17, 168

How to build up your bank account: 16, 164

How to buy or obtain NFTs: 171, 241

How to create (mint) an NFT: 171, 239

How to sell NFTs: 172, 239

Insurance, Chapter 4: 69, 192, 245

> **Healthcare, Part 2:** 89, 196

> **Insurance: Protecting Your Assets and Future:** 245

> **Liability Insurance:** 87, 195

> **Types of Insurance, Part 1:** 74, 194, 245

> **VA Benefits, Part 3:** 96, 197

Installment Loans: 114

Interest, Part 3: 131, 219

> **Interest rates:** 131, 148, 219, 229, 247

Interest rates and financial markets: 133, 223

Interest rates in the economy: 132, 222

Interest in Investing, Part 2: 147, 229

Investing, Chapter 6: 137, 224, 247

> **Investing: Growing Wealth for the Future:** 247

> **Interest in Investing, Part 2:** 147, 229

> **Positive Collections, Part 3:** 154, 234, 248

> **Types of Investment, Part 1:** 140, 227, 247

Liability Insurance: 87, 195

Loans, Chapter 5: 104, 197, 246

> **Applying for a federal student loan:** 116, 215

> **Applying for a non-federal student loan:** 116, 212

> **Auto loans:** 120, 232

> **Business expenses:** 120, 210

Car Loans: 119, 209, 232

Consolidating student loans: 120, 210

Cost of Money: 108, 202

Emergency expenses: 120

Getting a non-federal student loan: 117, 212

Hidden Fees: 110, 206

Home improvement: 120

Installment Loans: 114

Interest: 131, 219

Loans: Borrowing for Important Needs: 246

Medical expenses: 120

Mortgages: 128, 216, 232, 246

Moving expenses: 120, 210

Part 1: Types of Loans: 112, 209

Part 2: Uses of Loans: 119, 210

Passive Income: 248

Payday Loans: 115

Personal Loans: 122, 210, 232, 246

Receiving federal student loan funds: 117, 215

Revolving Loans: 113, 203

Secured Loan: 112, 209

Signing a Master Promissory Note (MPN): 117, 215

Student Loans: 116, 210, 233, 246

Types of Loans, Part 1: 112, 209

Unsecured Loans: 113, 203

Vacation: 120, 210

Medical expenses: 120

Money Market Accounts: 21, 173, 242

Money Orders: 32, 181

Mortgages: 128, 216, 232, 246

Moving expenses: 120, 210

Moving toward the Path to Financial Success, Chapter 7: 176, 241

Mutual Funds: 142, 226, 248

Non-Fungible Tokens (NFTs): 169, 238, 248

Opening a bank account: 9

Overdraft Fees: 17, 167

Passive Income: 248

Paying off debt (to build bank account): 16, 166

Payday Loans: 115

Personal Loans: 122, 210, 232, 246

Pitfalls of having a credit card: 59, 185

Positive Collections, Part 3: 154, 234, 248

Prime interest rates: 131, 220, 230

Real Estate Investing: 144, 226, 247

Receiving federal student loan funds: 117, 215

Revolving Loans: 113, 203

Saving (to build bank account): 16, 165

Savings Accounts: 22, 175, 242

Secured Loan: 112, 209

Signing a Master Promissory Note (MPN): 117, 215

So what specifically is the US Dollar?: 27, 178

Stocks: 140, 227, 247

Student Loans: 116, 210, 233, 246

Transaction alerts: 18

Types of Accounts, Part 3: 21, 173

Types of currency: 28, 178, 242

Types of Insurance, Part 1: 74, 194, 245

Types of Investment, Part 1: 140, 227, 247

Types of Loans, Part 1: 112, 209

Unsecured Loans: 113, 203

VA Benefits, Part 3: 96, 197

Vacation: 120, 210

Variable interest rates: 131, 220, 230, 247

Wedding expenses: 120, 210

www.ingramcontent.com/pod-product-compliance
Lightning Source LLC
Chambersburg PA
CBHW050004070726
47592CB00018B/775